LAST CALL

LAST CALL

POEMS ON ALCOHOLISM, ADDICTION, & DELIVERANCE

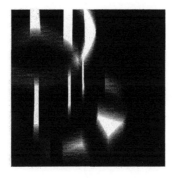

———— EDITED BY ————

SARAH GORHAM & JEFFREY SKINNER

SARABANDE BOOKS
LOUISVILLE, KENTUCKY

Managing Editor
Sarabande Books, Inc.
2234 Dundee Road, Suite 200
Louisville, KY 40205

LIBRARY OF CONGRESS CATALOGING-IN-PUBLICATION DATA

Last call : poems on alcoholism, addiction, and deliverance / edited by
Sarah Gorham and Jeffrey Skinner. —1st ed.
p.   cm.
ISBN 0-9641151-8-2 (alk. paper)
1. Alcoholism—Poetry.   2. Substance abuse—Poetry.
3. Alcoholism—Treatment—Poetry.   4. Substance Abuse—Treatment
—Poetry.   5. American poetry—20th century.   I. Gorham, Sarah,
1954–   . II. Skinner, Jeffrey.
PS595.A39L37   1997
811.008'0355—dc20   96-7251
CIP

Cover Painting: *Grief,* 1981, by Eric Fischl.
Oil on Canvas, 60" x 65".
Cincinnati Art Museum, gift of the RSM Company.
Reproduced with the kind permission of the artist.

Cover and interior design by Charles Casey Martin.

Manufactured in the United States of America.
This book is printed on acid-free paper.

Sarabande Books is a nonprofit literary organization.

To all those still suffering on the streets

CONTENTS

INTRODUCTION XI

JOAN LARKIN 25

    Good-bye 27
    Genealogy 28
    Co-alcoholic 29
    How the Healing Takes Place 30

THOMAS LUX 33

    Loudmouth Soup 35
    Amiel's Leg 36
    The Neighborhood of Make-Believe 37
    A Large Branch Splintered off a Tree in a Storm 38

MARTHA RHODES 39

    All the Soups 41
    His 42
    For Her Children 43
    A Small Pain 44
    Who Knew 45
    Sweeping the Floor 46

JANE MEAD 47

    On the Lawn at the Drug Rehab Center 49
    Fall 51
    The Memory 54
    Concerning That Prayer I Cannot Make 56

JEFFREY McDANIEL 59

    Disasterology 61

    Friends and High Places 63

    Modern Day Sisyphus 64

    1977 65

    First Person Omniscient 66

    The Multiple Floor 67

NANCY MITCHELL 69

    Love Story in Subtitles 71

    Runaway 73

    Incognito 74

    The Leaving 75

MARIE HOWE 77

    Recovery 79

    How Many Times 80

    The Mother 81

    The Promise 82

    The Dream 83

TESS GALLAGHER 85

    Even Now You Are Leaving 87

    3 A.M. Kitchen: My Father Talking 88

    Coming Home 90

    On Your Own 92

    Kidnaper 93

ETHERIDGE KNIGHT 95

    Welcome Back, Mr. Knight: Love of My Life 97

    Another Poem for Me (after Recovering from an O.D.) 99

    A Wasp Woman Visits a Black Junkie in Prison 100

    Feeling Fucked Up 102

CINDY GOFF 103

    Addiction 105
    I Feel Unattractive during Mating Season 106
    Drinking Beer with Sir 107
    Turning into an Oak Tree 108
    The First Sober Morning 109

LYNDA HULL 111

    Adagio 113
    Visiting Hour 115
    Lost Fugue for Chet 118

DENIS JOHNSON 121

    The Heavens 123
    The Honor 124
    The Words of a Toast 125

CINDY DAY ROBERTS 127

    The Leopard 129
    Poor Zelda 131
    Enough 133
    Let Go of It 135

WILLIAM LORAN SMITH 137

    The Family Man 139
    A Good Man's Fate 141
    Butchertown 142
    Sole of Dover 143

MICHAEL BURKARD 145

    Your Sister Life 147
    Woman in the Red House 149

Sober Ghost 150
The Summer after Last 152
How I Shaded the Book 153
But Beautiful 155

JEAN VALENTINE 159
The Summer Was Not Long Enough 161
American River Sky Alcohol Father 162
Everyone Was Drunk 163
The Drinker's Wife Writes Back 164
Night Lake 165
Forces 166
Trust Me 167
The River at Wolf 168

RAYMOND CARVER 169
Alcohol 171
NyQuil 173
Drinking While Driving 174
Luck 175
The Old Days 177
Gravy 179

CONTRIBUTORS' NOTES 181

THE EDITORS 187

ACKNOWLEDGMENTS 189

INTRODUCTION

I

I take wine to get rid of myself, to send myself away.
—Dr. Johnson

We can't say whether or not Dr. Johnson was an alcoholic, but he had it right: the alcoholic drinks, the drug addict shoots (or drops or smokes) to banish the self. It's not the *world* that's too much with the addict but the pressurized landscape within, which cannot be left behind, no matter how strong the promise of change held out by a new city or an exotic geography. Whether the hoped-for escape is Los Angeles or Sri Lanka, the self tags along. The addict eventually realizes that only a drink or a drug will transport the self to the realm of sleep and dreams, the addict's true destination. This realm, it's worth noting, was once known as the Land of Nod, where Cain journeyed after slaying Abel.

Of course, in the endgame of the illness, both "self" and "world" are subject to grim reduction. The *world* diminishes finally to a guarded supply house, the self to an instrument of forced entry; there is only the addict and his or her drug of choice. But in spite of much interesting postmodern speculation about the insubstantial nature of the "self" (which seems to conclude that our old notion is a ruse, a socially constructed emptiness), anyone who has observed an addict's progressive deterioration knows that *something* is draining away—something that once defined the addict as an individual human being. "Every junkie," Neil Young sang, "is like a setting sun."

Absence. Loss of self, or a macabre living experiment on *whatever* might constitute the self. The destruction from within of a world both personal and social...

What great subjects for poetry!

And yet when my coeditor Sarah Gorham and I began looking for precedents, for previous collections on the subject of alcoholism and drug addiction, we found—none. There were anthologies of poems on Barbie dolls and pet dogs, on baseball, tennis, horror films, on various disabilities, on AIDS. There were collections of sestinas, sonnets, prose poems. There were yards of poetry anthologies on nearly every subject one could think of, but none we could find on a disease that had ruined the lives and talents of a multitude of twentieth-century poets: Dylan Thomas, Edward Arlington Robinson, Hart Crane, Edna St. Vincent Millay, Dorothy Parker, Robert Lowell, Elizabeth Bishop, Theodore Roethke, John Berryman, Anne Sexton, to name a few....This is, of course, not to mention the prose writers, including five of the seven native-born American Nobel Prize winners in literature: Sinclair Lewis, Eugene O'Neill, William Faulkner, Ernest Hemingway, and John Steinbeck.

No wonder alcoholism has been called "the writers' disease."

2

Alcoholism and drug addiction are persistent human phenomena. Every literate culture that has had access to alcohol and/or mood-altering substances records the miserable effects of excessive use: "No, I don't approve of drinking," Aristophanes wrote, in *The Wasps;* "I know what wine leads to: breaches of the peace, assault and battery—and a fine to pay before you've got rid of the hangover."

There are warnings about the evils of drink and of drunkards in the Koran, in major Buddhist texts, and in the Bible. Ecclesiastes, for example—"Shew not thy valiantness in wine; for wine hath destroyed many" (34:25, 29). Folklore from a range of cultures offers similar bits of undeluded wisdom evolved through long experience with abuse. Many can quote the Japanese adage, "First the man takes a drink, then the drink takes a drink, then the drink takes the man." And the tragedy that can issue from "too much of a good thing" is not always a thing hidden from history, or limited to the personal and the local: "Drunkenness, the most illiberal, but not the most dangerous, of *our* vices, was sometimes capable, in a less civilized state of mankind, of occasioning a battle, a war, or a revolution" (Edward Gibbon, *The History of the Decline and Fall of the Roman Empire).*

One could go on. The salient point is the remarkable consistency over time, and across lines of race, class, gender, and ethnicity, to the pattern of self-and-other-destructiveness caused by "substance abuse."

And yet the majority of people can drink moderately and *not* get into trouble. They can use alcohol, and other mood-altering drugs, to relax, to be sociable, to heighten their enjoyment of conversation and fellowship. And then they can leave it alone. They do not find themselves obsessing about the next drink or drug, ordering their lives around the opportunity to get high again. They do not have the feeling, after one drink, or seven drinks, that they have finally come home, relieved of an oppressive and continuous dull fear stretching back into childhood.

Precisely because for the vast majority of people who take a drink the effect is so modest and peripheral, *they* do not need to base their lives on an intricate system of lies and deception.

The alcoholic and drug addict are different. For them the drug of choice begins as a revelation: a coping mechanism they never had, a buffer, a chemical pillow. "I was born," says Clancy, a self-declared alcoholic in recovery, "without emotional insulation." For the addict, alcohol and drugs are useful substances: they work, they have value. And in some instances junk or booze can facilitate years of productive, responsible behavior, a convincing imitation of normalcy, as in the case of what's known as a "functioning alcoholic."

The problem is that the substance of salvation grows voracious in its claim on the addict's body and soul. Supply and access to it become first priority, superseding responsibilities to family, work, and conscience. What began as a welcome solution mutates into a case of blackmail in which the stakes are exponentially raised, until the addict no longer needs a drug to get through life, but needs it to live. It is, of course, at the same time killing him or her.

And it may well be killing others also. Fifty to eighty percent of all major crimes are drug- or alcohol-related. Half the people in state prisons for committing violent crimes report they were under the influence of alcohol or drugs at the time of offense.

The statistics keep coming: one out of four Americans experiences family problems related to alcohol abuse; half of all traffic fatalities are alcohol-related; alcohol abuse plays a part in one out of three failed marriages. The yearly costs, in terms of productivity loss, treatment, and crime: alcohol, $92 billion; drugs, $67 billion....

It is a problem somewhat like the weather: everyone talks about it, but no one, it seems, does anything. But not for lack of trying. We are disturbed by the statistics on crime and failed marriages and highway fatalities and, being American and therefore essentially pragmatic, we want to "fix" the problem; we want to raise the hood and get to work. The two main approaches today—punishment (and control of substance supply) and treatment—have for a long time been the only perceived alternatives. Like all other current American "issues," what to do about addiction has become highly politicized, and each of these methods has energetic and vocal proponents. Some measures have helped. Stricter laws concerning DUI violations, for example, have apparently resulted in fewer mortalities due to drunk driving.

And yet there remains a core of users—for example, the ten percent of the population that consumes half of all alcohol sold in the country—whose number seems stubbornly fixed. And the enormous costs continue.

3

Many of the statistics in this introduction were drawn from a report entitled *Substance Abuse: The Nation's Number One Health Problem*, prepared in 1993 by the Institute for Health Policy at Brandeis University for The Robert C. Wood Foundation. It is easy, given the obvious breadth and depth of human suffering caused by substance abuse, to assert that it is indeed the *nation's number one health problem*, and periodically an article surfaces making just this point. Recently one appeared in the *New York Times*, written by former Secretary of Health, Education, and Welfare, Joseph Califano. It was entitled *It's Drugs, Stupid*, a wittily aggressive play on the Clinton campaign slogan. After reading the article, which made the radical suggestion that instead of focusing on crime, poverty, and health-care costs, we should be attacking a major cause of all three—drug and alcohol abuse—Sarah and I eagerly awaited the storm of letters and op-ed pieces such incendiary articles typically provoke.

There weren't any, at least none that were published. But then, Califano himself had forecast this indifference in the article: "For 30 years, America has tried to curb crime…health costs…and welfare systems….All the while, we have undermined these efforts with our personal and national denial about the sinister dimension drug abuse and addiction have added to our society."

Denial, as the now familiar Stuart Smalley joke goes, is not a river in Egypt. We have more information about drugs—in the press, in the schools, and in the air—than we can process. It *seems* to be a subject that has finally moved out of the realm of taboo and into the well-lighted arena of public discourse.

But Califano is right. No one really wants to talk about it.

The obituary of the movie star who was, to anyone who knew him slightly, an obvious drunk, says he died of "gastrointestinal infection," or "heart failure," or "pulmonary edema"—something, anything that does not mention alcohol or drugs. The paper reports this because this is what the star's doctor said, which is what the star's family wanted the doctor to say. And on it goes, the same unspoken principle operating for the less exhalted professions, for plumbers and writers in small towns and big cities. A recent survey of Americans found that respondents would, given the odious choice, much rather be known as "mentally ill" than "alcoholic."

Why? Why are we as a nation and as individuals so loath to consider alcohol and drugs as causal factors in our failures, and to admit how often they are responsible, indirectly—or more often than we dream, *directly*—for the ruin and death of "good people"? Why does the stigma, in spite of a deluge of talk, and the obvious improvement in treatment methods, remain?

I suspect that the answer is our deep ambivalence about what we believe alcoholism and drug addiction to be. Despite all our well-intentioned rhetoric we cannot fully accept the American Medical Association's designation of alcoholism as a "disease"; we feel intuitively that there must be a fundamental difference between death from cancer and death from alcoholic cirrhosis or an overdose of heroin.

Why did Mickey Mantle receive a transplant, when there must have been someone more deserving, someone who *had no part* in his own body's rebellion? We think this, but we don't say it. We have been told by health-care "experts" that alcoholism is not a matter of weak will or flawed moral character. But the experts cannot give us a complete and rational alternative to our intuitive conclusions. The fact that a man so fabulously gifted and accomplished could destroy himself and those around him through the act of habitually drinking too damn much simply does not make sense. There is no reason in it at all.

If he could not help himself, all right, we sigh. A victim of circumstance. A disease. We are used, these days, to thinking in such terms. —But what can it mean, that he could not help himself? Surely no one forced the glass to *Mickey Mantle's* lips....

Maybe it *is* genetic. Things seem to be tending that way. Every few months or years one hears a news report that scientists are close to identifying "alcoholic genes." Studies of twins strongly indicate that at the very least the predisposition to alcoholism is inherited.

And if it is proven to be in the genes, then what? When we know that addiction is a trait like blue eyes, will that remove the mystery? When technology progresses to the point where we can *fix* those faulty genes in utero, will we?

Addiction has been compared to an elephant sitting in the living room, which family members do their level best to step around. What I've tried to do in the preceding paragraphs is to dramatize our conflicted thoughts, our unresolved questions, and our feelings about addiction. The circularity and sad inconclusiveness of our reasoning on the subject may help explain our national reluctance to pursue it, to willingly consider with such people as Joseph Califano why it is that addiction is so deeply implicated in the core problems we face as a society. We seem to be at an impasse: science, religion, and all manner of social discourse have tried and failed to formulate a practical answer to the problem of addiction. And yet the elephant remains, taking up more and more living space.

My intention here is not to endorse any of the existent theories or remedies, nor to propose new ones, but to suggest that the subject is indeed as complex and ambiguous as we feel it to be—and to suggest that this is not necessarily a wrong or a bad thing. Perhaps if we could relax our impulse to either fix or ignore the phenomenon of addiction for a period and simply spend some time with the elephant, as if we were wholly and contentedly ignorant of its ontology, something interesting, even valuable, might happen.

4

Both Sarah and I have personal stakes in issues of sobriety and addiction. To say more than this, we feel, would be an imprudence that might lead to some harm. It is for similar reasons that we must make clear that inclusion of any author in this collection says nothing about his or her status vis-à-vis addiction or alcoholism.

What appearance in the anthology does mean is that in our opinion the poet has something essential to say on the subject, and says it in lively and distinctive language. It was important to us that each poem we chose first be successful *as poem,* as compelling verbal object. We realize that such a criterion is in some measure subjective, but we are proud of the poems assembled here, and will stand by our choices.

Because of our interest, we had over the years been alert to poems which had something to say on addiction. We began by soliciting authors with whom we were already familiar, including a request that each suggest other poets whose work might be right for *Last Call.* The result is a collection that mixes the work of well-known figures such as Etheridge Knight, Ray Carver, Tess Gallagher, Denis Johnson, and others, with exciting newer voices—Jane Mead, Jeffrey McDaniel, and Cindy Day Roberts, to mention three. And while we don't claim that the present volume is definitive or the last poetic word on the subject, we are pleased that it includes a variety of styles, tones, and points of view.

The latter seemed to us especially important, since alcoholism and drug addiction are known, with good reason, as "family diseases." Thus we learn from Jane Mead's poem "On the Lawn at the Drug Rehab Center" how the family must endure the addict's terrifying and unpredictable shuttle between sentimentality and rage:

You say our faces,
the night we came to lock you up,
made a beautiful circle
around you. And then you stop
and I see it coming—"What
do you want from me anyway, you fucking
kidnappers?" I'll tell you. Exactly.
I want you to tell the truth—
our faces were *not* beautiful.

We witness the courage of refusal to accept the shifting of blame in Jean Valentine's "The Drinker's Wife Writes Back": "...how could I ever have told/ anyone how it was, how the lighted house/ went out in the gin brightness/ you called 'the war'—and that I did this to you—/ I did not do this...." We see the chaos of an alcoholic family, the isolation a child feels between the slammed doors and thrown dishes, the mother passed out on the couch, the father and the sisters leaving, always leaving, while the speaker as child sits in a metal chair, "...waiting for one person/ hungry enough to come home" (Martha Rhodes, "All the Soups"). We admire the imaginative bravery of Tess Gallagher's "3 A.M. Kitchen: My Father Talking," in which the poet adopts the laconic voice of her father; and behind the bare-bones story of a life spent essentially withdrawn from those he loved, we feel the weight of what's unsaid straining under the poem's surface.

In Lynda Hull's startling poems on Hart Crane and Chet Baker, the romance of art going down under its own power (and the power of addiction) is both embodied and unmasked: *"...this is the tied-off vein, this is 3 A.M. terror/ thrumming, this is the carnation of blood clouding/ the syringe...."* Marie Howe tells of the difficulty of living *without* drugs: "Can we endure it, the rain finally stopped?" ("Recovery"). Similarly, Michael Burkard describes the temptation to look back: "And being an alcoholic, even in recovery, I have/ this more than momentary sense that dark life isn't so bad after all./ There is an alcoholic shine to that darkness." No one's career plans include becoming an addict, as Denis Johnson knows: "Soon after this I became/ another person, somebody/ I would have brushed off if I'd met him that night,/ somebody I never imagined" ("The Honor").

Voices vary widely, though the subject is one, from the antic surrealism of Jeffrey McDaniel in "Disasterology"—"My life's a chandelier dropped from an airplane"—to the raw explicitness of Joan Larkin's "I come from alcohol./ I was set down in it like a spark in gas."

There's rich irony, at once jaunty and dead serious, in Tom Lux's "Loudmouth Soup": "We'll have *a* drink/ and talk, we'll have/ *a* drink and sleep, we'll/ have *a* drink/ and die, grim-about-it-with-piquancy." And in contrast there's the subtle hush of Cindy Day Roberts's "Enough," where the addict's typical excess of self-regard is used to see, finally, through the eyes of others, the center widened to include all the heartbreaking stories that make up our lives, ending in forgiveness: "It was a story the night told:/ I am enough just as I am—that/ is what the eternal sky said./ And the man, woman and child—/ we are all enough."

Etheridge Knight's tongue-in-cheek self-interrogation, "Welcome Back, Mr. Knight: Love of My Life," is filled with the fierce energy that sometimes blooms at the end of the line, the sudden moral awareness that snaps on like a harsh light in the addict's darkroom, and is accompanied by, of all things, humor: "Welcome back, Mr. K: Love of My Life—/ How's your drinking problem? —your thinking/ Problem? you/ are/ pickling/ Your liver—/ Gotta / watch / out for the/ 'Ol Liver': Love of My Life." And there is Ray Carver, with his extraordinary gift for facing the clear fact and rendering it in heartbreakingly certain terms: "Years later,/ I still wanted to give up/ friends, love, starry skies,/ for a house where no one/ was home, no one coming back,/ and all I could drink" ("Luck").

5

We offer this anthology in part because we believe poetry provides a fresh and open-ended context within which to consider alcoholism and drug abuse. As I've implied, public discourse on the subject has settled into well-worn grooves, and the tendency of talks at the level of state policy is toward clear, employable solutions: it's bad behavior—lock 'em up; it's a disease—sober 'em up. We think the desire to reduce a complex issue, which has caused so much heartache, to manageable dimensions is completely understandable. The world of the addict, however, is one of contradiction and paradox, in recovery as well as in the practicing phase.

Perhaps more so in recovery. To gain any progress toward redemption the addict must accept, must live within, a number of paired statements that are both true and contradictory on their face:

Addiction is a disease, and the behavior it led to out of my control/
I must make amends for the trouble I caused

I can stay clean and sober a lifetime/ I have a daily reprieve from addiction

The idea of living within contradiction and paradox is a familiar one for the poet. Keat's idea of *negative capability,* which he defines as a state of being in which one "is capable of being in uncertainties, mysteries, doubts, without any irritable reaching after fact and reason...of remaining content with half knowledge," describes very well the poet's necessary humility before the language. To be open to receiving the unexpected, poets must give up, or at least suspend, all they think they know for sure. This condition of spiritual submission, or readiness, is remarkably similar to the stance suggested by Alcoholics Anonymous for recovering addicts, who must "give up all our old ideas," and for whom "The result was nil until we let go absolutely."

Carl Jung, in a letter to Bill Wilson, the founder of AA, said that the alcoholic's "craving for alcohol was the equivalent on a low level of the spiritual thirst of our being for wholeness, expressed in medieval language: the union with God." Jung wrote this letter shortly before he died, in the early 1960s. He was well aware of how silly such an assertion would sound to a great majority of the educated and, in fact, the above quotation was followed immediately by the caveat, "How could one formulate such an insight in a language that is not misunderstood in our days?"

Perhaps even more in our present day would "the union with God" be cause for skepticism and misunderstanding. We live in a literal age, an age of nonfiction prose. Few believe the imagination worth attention, unless it result in a movie, a spectacular slam-dunk, a trillion-dollar merger, an Elvis-sighting. Books with the word "soul" in the title do a brisk business, but we Americans have always had a taste for easy enlightenment, and one gets the feeling that this interest is merely the latest permutation of the search for "fitness": ethereal self-help, Velcro wrist-weights for the spirit. American monasteries, Catholic and Buddhist, are not swelling with people willing to give twenty years or more to the "care of the soul."

And yet poems keep getting written that attempt to limn the border between the body's outline in time and space and all that lies beyond. And addicts keep recovering through a shift in awareness, a turning away from materialism and obsession with the self, to trust in a benevolent creator—no matter the form or name—and a revelatory, compassionate openness to others.

What both projects have in common is trust in the invisible and faith that the products of spiritual work are additions to reality. Poets and addicts know from experience the difficulty of such work, how it refuses to bend to the will, how unexpected grace seems when it arrives and the poem writes itself, or the addict is suddenly filled with gratitude, and feels the universe owes him, or her, nothing.

We do not claim for this book anything so grand as a solution to the nation's substance abuse problem. But we do believe that poetry can help, as it has in the past. It is entirely possible that many poets of Lowell's generation, for example, stayed alive as long as they did *because* of their engagement with the creative force of poetry, in spite of the inevitable decline caused by addiction. We hope that the poems in this book will, first, give readers the unique pleasures of language well used—we consider the pleasure of poetry in itself an affirmation of human life. But it is also our hope that the poems provide a valuable kind of "news" on the much discussed but little understood subject of addiction. I speak of the news William Carlos Williams had in mind in these lines:

> ...Look at
> what passes for the new
> You will not find it there but in
> despised poems.
> It is difficult
> to get the news from poems
> yet men die miserably every day
> for lack
> of what is found there.

This passage has often been used to underline the importance of art to human experience. As such it is an eloquent metaphor for the soul-hunger that transcends our need for daily bread and shelter. But it is rarely argued that Williams was speaking of literal death from a shortage of poems, or from whatever news might be contained within them. We die in any case, miserably or not.

Addiction, however, is a sickness that inextricably blends the physical and spiritual, and as such is both symbol of spiritual longing and a horrifying reality, the cause of immense sadness. Attempts to understand and control its devastation have been inconclusive at best. News from the street, at this point, is more of the same, and uniformly bad. We have grown used to turning away.

But there is another kind of understanding, too little considered, which is a redemptive force at work daily in thousands of lives. This type of understanding is experiential and resists analysis or reduction to simple formula. Like poetry, it accepts the double realm, the apparent fact of our suspension between the seen and the unseen. It embraces difficulty. Williams had it right: we need the news of "despised poems" if we are to be fully human, if we are to live and die as something more than animals. And in the border where poetry and addiction coexist, that place where *Last Call* resides, the news of poetry might call back a banished self, might literally save a life.

—*Jeffrey Skinner*

LAST CALL

JOAN
LARKIN

Good-bye

You are saying good-bye to your last
drink. There is no lover
like her: bourbon, big gem
in your palm and steep
fiery blade in your throat,
deadeye down. None like her
but her sister, first
gin, like your first
seaswim, first woman
whose brine took to your tongue,
who could change the seasons of your cells
like nothing else.
Unless it was wine, finally
your only companion, winking
across the table, hinting
in her rubies, her first-class labels,
of her peasant blood
and the coarse way she would open you.

Good-bye, beauties. You don't want to say it.
You try to remember
the night you fell out of the car
and crawled to the curb, the night
two of you stood
screaming over your daughter's crib.
You remember deaths
by gin, by easy capsules—
the friend who fell in silence
and the friend who quoted *Antony* in his suicide note.
All this helps for a moment, till your heart
blooms and stiffens with desire.

Genealogy

I come from alcohol.
I was set down in it like a spark in gas.
I lay down dumb with it, I let it erase what it liked.
I played house with it, let it dress me, undress me.
I exulted, I excused.
I married it. And where it went, I went.
I gave birth to it.
I nursed, I plotted murder with it.
I laid its table, paid its promises.
I lived with it wherever it liked to live:
in the kitchen, under the bed, at the coin laundry,
out by the swings, in the back seat of the car,
at the trashed Thanksgiving table.
I sat with it in the blear of TV.
I sat where it glittered, carmine,
where it burned in a blunt glass,
where it stood in a glittering lineup on the bar.
I saw it in the dull mirror, making up my face,
in the weekend silence,
in the smashed dish, in the slammed car door,
in the dead husband, the love.
Alcohol in the torn journal.
Alcohol in the void mirror.
My generations are of alcohol
and all that I could ever hope to bear.

Co-alcoholic

I saw you in the street, head lowered, stumbling;
I waited two years to call.
This is the last time, I told myself.
Unless he's dead, I'll tell him about the fellowship.
This time, no ice against glass against my ear—
"I'm sober," you said.

You were trembling, pallid,
your fat a cradle around you,
the old tattoo like a bruise purpling your arm.
You kept trying to kiss me.
"I need someone I don't have to impress," you said.
Should. Shouldn't. I judged myself without pity.

You remembered 1969, an acid trip,
the *I Ching* hexagrams we'd formed, fucking.
Above, the clinging, fire; below, wind and wood.
Lake over fire: molting, an animal's pelt.
Last night, the rose and bruise-purple of my cunt
were the colors in my mind's eye

of slick internal shapes twisting and coupling,
Blake's underworld river, looped like a gut.
Above, the abysmal, water,
below, the receptive, earth—
hair glistening like oil
on your thin chest my breasts wilted on.
Last night the fear in my eyes stared at the fear in your eyes.

How the Healing Takes Place

How the face changes, the cloud
you'd skim from a pot of lentils
comes clear, how the gaze
comes clear as honey when you hear it,
how the eyes surrender their fear,
dark lake of beach plums
boiled for jam. How flesh

yields new flesh, lips
softening like soaked beans.
How the puffed skin settles,
dough becomes bread,
its brown, delicate grain.
How the dead hair—that mouse,
matted and stiff in the trap—
grows sleek again. How the thoughts,

like black ants going
and coming from the mouse's corpse,
go slower. How the torn mind
puts forth tendrils.
How the gray house of the lungs,
frayed and weather-beaten,
fills with moist breath.
How the breath brings healing

to all parts of the body.
To the salt rivers of blood,
to the many-tiered skeleton,
to the breast, beaded and creased,
humming like wings in the jewelweed,
to the softening belly,
to the thick, unfurling petals of the sex.

How everything speaks—
hands unclenching—
heart.
How the belly will lift its flat
stone, the tears roll
stones from entrances.

THOMAS
LUX

Loudmouth Soup

Vodka, whisky, gin. Scotch. Red wine, cognac,
brandy—are you getting thirsty yet?—ale,
rye. It all tastes good: on the rocks, with a splash,
side of soda, shaken
not stirred, triple
olives, one of those nutritious little pearl
onions, a double, neat,
with a twist. Drink
it up, let's have a drink: dry beer, wet beer,
light, dark, and needled beer. Oh parched,
we drank the river
nearly to its bed at times, and were so numb
a boulder on a toe
was pleasant pain, all pain
was pleasant since that's all there was, pain,
and everything that was deeply felt, deeply,
was not. Bourbon, white and pink wine, *apéritif,*
cordial (hardly!), cocktail, martini,
highball, *digestif,* port, grain
punch—are you getting thirsty yet?—line them up!
We'll have *a* drink
and talk, we'll have
a drink and sleep, we'll
have *a* drink
and die, grim–about–it–with–piquancy.
It was a long time on the waiting list
for zero
and I'm happy
for the call out of that line
to other, less predictable,
more joyful
slides to ride on home.

Amiel's Leg

We were in a room that was once an attic,
the tops of the trees filled the windows, a breeze
crossed the table where we sat
and Amiel, about age four, came to visit
with her father, my friend,
and it was spring I think, and I remember
being happy—her mother was there too,
and my wife, and a few other friends.
It was spring, late spring, because the trees
were full but still that slightly lighter
green; the windows were open,
some of them, and I'll say it
out loud: I was happy, sober, at the time childless
myself, and it was one
of those moments: just like that, Amiel
climbed on my lap and put her head back against my chest.
I put one hand on her knees
and my other hand on top of that hand.
That was all, that was it.
Amiel's leg was cool, faintly rubbery.
We were there—I wish I knew the exact
date, time—and that
was all, that was it.

The Neighborhood of Make-Believe

To go there: do not fall asleep, your forehead
on the footstool; do not have
your lunchpail dreams
or dreams so peaceful you hear leaves thud
into the fine silt at a river's edge;
do not hope you'll find it on this updraft
or that downdraft
in the airy airlessness.
It is elsewhere, elsewhere, the neighborhood you seek.
The neighborhood you long for,
where the gentle trolley—*ding, ding*—passes
through, where the adults are kind
and, better, sane,
that neighborhood is gone, no, never
existed, though it should have
and had a chance once
in the hearts of women, men (farmers dreamed
this place, and teachers, book writers, oh thousands
of workers, mothers prayed for it, hunchbacks,
nurses, blind men, maybe most of all soldiers,
even a few generals, millions
through the millennia...), some of whom,
despite anvils on their chests,
despite taking blow after blow across shoulders and necks,
despite derision and scorn,
some of whom still, *still*
stand up every day against ditches swollen with blood,
against ignorance, still dreaming,
full-fledged adults, still fighting,
trying to build a door to that place,
trying to pry open the ugly,
bullet-pocked, and swollen gate
to the other side,
the neighborhood of make-believe.

A Large Branch Splintered off a Tree in a Storm

and was hurled to the ground like a spear.
In the morning there it stood, upright,
a new tree, twenty feet tall, sprung overnight.
Torn off with such force
it impales by several inches the grass and earth

and as I haul it out
I think: What if this very spot,
what were the chances—mathematically, spatially,
time-of-day-wise, cosmically—what odds
this spot could have been my wife's heart,

my baby's fontanel? Normal thinking
or normal (slash) paranoid?
I pull the branch—the white pith
of the wood stained by the wet earth—out,
bending to grip it at the base,

it was that deep. Torn from its source,
its leaves just beginning to wilt,
their gray backs closing like fists
around the greener fronts.
And then with my hatchet I hacked it up.

MARTHA
RHODES

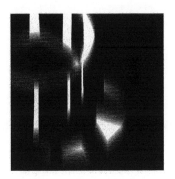

All the Soups

All the soups I've made in my life—
slow-cooking easy broths, red thick
puréed blends. Churning it all up
alone in my kitchen, tasting,
covering, uncovering, remembering
spat-out carrots pinched between Mother's fingers
and pressed back into my mouth, Mother
wanting to get done with those meals, running
upstairs before Father comes home, Father
grubbing through drawers looking for pints,
both sisters up in the field getting plastered
and laid, me stuck in that chair,
locked behind a metal tray, not knowing
who's slamming the screen door so hard
that waves in my milk cup spill to my lap.
There's always a pot of soup on the stove.
I trace cats and houses on the damp kitchen wall,
waiting for anyone to come home,
waiting for one person
hungry enough to come home.

His

He finds the dusty gin,
pours a double, straight,
then another. Lunch will be fast.
He'll sleep after, there,
on the sofa. I'll watch him.

It's mostly my mouth that's his,
and my hair, thinning,
pushing back from my brow, exposing
me, like him.

Oh, I've known since I was seven,
since then I've known I was him,
his.

For Her Children

She pretends to be dead
and unless you creep up and pinch her someplace tender
you think she really is dead.

Then she gets up—
refreshed now, pink-cheeked,
her hair a little sweaty.

Those short bursts of lightness after sleep—
the noiseless house, bright and aired,
the children butterflies,
delighted when she scoops them up in her net.

For them, she does not move
and they must not wake her
and they must not pinch her ever again.

A Small Pain

It's true she liked it.
Mostly when it hurt, a little.
Just a little made it good.
And still does. It's better
if it hurts just a little bit.

So when she buys jeans, they're tight
and she feels their tightness everywhere.
Just a little tight, a small pain.

And when her forehead's hot,
her throat sore, she smokes more cigarettes.
When the soles of her shoes wear thin,
she wears them another season,
till the dents in her heels from the little nail heads
grow hard and red. And when her husband stops talking,
stops holding her hand and tickling her thigh,
stops coming home every night, stops calling her,
stops stopping by, she stays, she stays.
It is winter. The boiler just broke, the blankets
have fallen off the bed. She stays
until she gets a little colder,
just a little colder.

Who Knew

She was crying in the kitchen.
I didn't want breakfast.
She hadn't made breakfast,
just a half-frozen lump of juice
in my glass and a spoon.
"He's cheating on me."
I knew and knew with whom.

What dishes would break,
what pills would she take,
why would she write such a long note
then snip it and snip it
into the kitchen pail?
I drank the juice and ran to school.

Tire marks through my hopscotch grid,
all the doors unlocked, she'd left
my two suitcases unpacked,
untouched under my bed.
Who knew when she'd be back?
Who cared if she was dead.

She called when he got home,
when I was in my room,
her letter, pages of blurry tears
pasted together in my drawer,
his voice, a drunken palm
begging at my door.

Sweeping the Floor

She loves especially the Cha Cha Cha,
her right foot crossing her left
in a daring twist. And sometimes
she tangos wall to wall across the room.
This makes her laugh.

She knows she isn't graceful.
She shuts her eyes to mirrors
and any shiny surface. Years ago,
at a cousin's wedding, someone whispered
in her ear, Dancing with you,
my God, dancing with you,
is like pushing around a piano.

And sometimes when she's dancing fast,
can barely stop, doesn't want to stop,
can't catch her breath, feels very hot,
she gives herself a hug, a squeeze,
a spin, a dip so low her hair,
her short wispy hair seems to brush the floor,
it glides on the floor, it sweeps the floor.

JANE
MEAD

On the Lawn at the Drug Rehab Center

To my father

Because the wooden lawn statues
here—the bear "whose tail
could be an emerging turd" says Gale,
the squatting monkey, the cow
with taut udders—are all vaguely
obscene, this lawn is not quite
institutional. We sit, half a family
in a circle, Gale, Richie and I
—with our father, dad—groping
awkwardly back to each other.

You ask our ages: we are
older than you thought, much.
You offer us each a small cigar
and ask if we are happy.

The blue smoke turns to water
in my lungs. Gale brings out
the pornographic comics she's working on,
in which her history teacher
meets an embarrassing end.
The teacher's kidnapped—ransom set.
Nobody pays. The ransom is reduced
and reduced again. It would be awful—
ransom demanded and nobody
so much as notices. We laugh.

You say our faces,
the night we came to lock you up,
made a beautiful circle
around you. And then you stop
and I see it coming—"What
do you want from me anyway, you fucking
kidnappers?" I'll tell you. Exactly.

I want you to tell the truth—
our faces were *not* beautiful.
Truth is you fired five shots
and we scattered. Behind the stone
pillar between the vineyard
and the house I thought, that night,
of how you taught us, years ago,
to stand quietly among the vines,
to close our eyes and listen
with our feet to the sound
of the grapes growing. I listened
and I didn't hear them, father.
I heard the words
I'd read on intervention theory—
"Tell the addict how he has
let you down. Have specific
examples ready." Useless.
But we went after you again.

I know there are rooms in the mind
anyone can walk into—
I'm not saying they're any worse
than this strange lawn,
or any better,
but if you want to march
methodically into that complicated
place, I want you
to stand up first, to shake my hand
and say good-bye.

Fall

for Aspen and Shaheen

This morning I found
a used needle in the empty box
marked *produce* in the empty
icebox, sponged the blood speck
from its tip. The fog pushed at the windows
with a sickening heave. I picked
another moth from the drain.

To pick a moth from a sink
for the pain its flight might waken
in the mind's tepid stagnation
is a desperate act.
But last night I sat on the concrete floor
watching flies on the toilet seat,
and listened to my father, who was up
in the loft breathing hayseed
and waving his .38 at the place
where the north star should have been—
shouting at my cousin who'd gone down
to Santa Cruz with scabs
the size of nickels on her feet
to trade her baby for someone's Porsche,
and I have forgotten
what it is to be human.
What it is to be human:
I forget the dusted wings, the whiff
of sage on the fog; I forget
that an action could be made
to make meaning.

Did I choose
the humiliation of my own blood,
this hiding in shirtsleeves?

If this moth could shock me
I might remember that half-thought
before I smoked my first cigarette
at the top of the vineyard
fifteen years ago—that split
second when I sensed
I was choosing—or that fleeting
tug the first night I rummaged
in the tack room for a horse needle.

There is a strange world
in the changing of a light bulb,
the waxing of a bookshelf
I think I could grow by,
as into a dusty dream
in which each day layers
against one just past
and molds the one to come,
content as cabbage
drudging towards harvest.

It may be too far
to get to.
This morning my sister's children
knocked on the door—
I said I was sleeping; my eyes
were crusted wild and they said "but
Aunt Jane, we don't have
mud on our feet, please
can't we come in?"

Their terrifying, trusting voices
come back and back.

If I stepped outside
now, I could watch them
pedaling up and down
the foggy rows of vines,
their eyes clear

and open wide. Someday
I would like to write something
beautiful for them,
a song of order, undrunk,
but livable, a song
of frogs tonguing into themselves
the quiet deaths of flies, of nights
needing days, a song
equal to this season.

The Memory

The body refuses to die.
The soul refuses to be stronger.
The memory I cannot fully form
will never fully leave me—
the memory of a man who tried to save me:
vague curve of shoulders and back
disappearing down the playground path
between snowdrifts. Swingchains
on my hands in winter.

Come back—there must be something
you must have forgotten—.

Did he wear a red scarf?
Was he shoeless in the snow?
He had a three day's beard—or, no—
he was clean-shaven. He bent over.
With his warm breath he unfroze
my hands from the swingchains—
not pulling till they were ready.

If only he would tell me now:
What does it mean to let go?

Sometimes a strange feeling comes over me.
My body tingles as if it were alone
with the soul, trying to explain to her
its inability. She understands.
She needs something.

Why is she not complete?
What does she need to be complete?
Ask the present, ask the body. No,
ask the blurred snowdrift darkening, quick—
ask the child on the swingset; she knows.

It was a red scarf.
Yes, and the wind blew it as he bent over
and the knees of his unbelted pants were baggy.
His breath loosened my hands from the chains,
from the swingset. He whispered
"let go."

Then he turned and walked sadly
down the playground path and suddenly,
in the tired curve of a back,
my body recognized itself.

Nothing more. Nothing forgotten.

It seems wrong—
the way the body refuses to die.
It seems wrong—
the way the soul refuses to be stronger.

There should have been something more.
A binding word perhaps—*body, sorrow*—
or a parting glance dissolving—
too late, too late, too late.

But now, at least, there is nothing
between me and my soul but myself.

Concerning That Prayer I Cannot Make

Jesus, I am cruelly lonely
and I do not know what I have done
nor do I suspect that you will answer me.

And, what is more, I have spent
these bare months bargaining
with my soul as if I could make her
promise to love me when now it seems
that what I meant when I said "soul"
was that the river reflects
the railway bridge just as the sky
says it should—it speaks *that* language.

I do not know who you are.

I come here every day
to be beneath this bridge,
to sit beside this river,
so I *must* have seen the way
the clouds just slide
under the rusty arch—
without snagging on the bolts,
how they are borne along on the dark water—
I must have noticed their fluent speed
and also how that tattered blue T-shirt
remains snagged on the crown
of the mostly sunk dead tree
despite the current's constant pulling.
Yes, somewhere in my mind there must
be the image of a sky blue T-shirt, caught,
and the white islands of ice flying by
and the light clouds flying slowly
under the bridge, though today the river's
fully melted. I must have seen.

But I did not see.

I am not equal to my longing.
Somewhere there should be a place
the exact shape of my emptiness—
there should be a place
responsible for taking one back.
The river, of course, has no mercy—
it just lifts the dead fish
toward the sea.

Of course, of course.

What I *meant* when I said "soul"
was that there should be a place.

On the far bank the warehouse lights
blink red, then green, and all the yellow
machines with their rusted scoops and lifts
sit under a thin layer of sunny frost.

And look—
my own palm—
there, slowly rocking.
It is *my* pale palm—
palm where a black pebble
is turning and turning.

> Listen—
> all you bare trees
> burrs
> brambles
> pile of twigs
> red and green lights flashing
> muddy bottle shards
> shoe half buried—listen

> listen, I am holy.

JEFFREY
McDANIEL

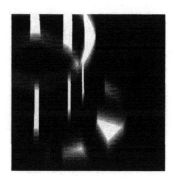

Disasterology

The Badger is the thirteenth astrological sign.
My sign. The one the other signs evicted: unanimously.

So what?! Think I want to read about my future
in the newspaper next to the comics?

My third grade teacher told me I had no future.
I run through snow and turn around
just to make sure I've got a past.

My life's a chandelier dropped from an airplane.
I graduated first in my class from alibi school.

There ought to be a healthy family cage at the zoo,
or an open field, where I can lose my mother
as many times as I need.

When I get bored, I call the cops, tell them
there's a pervert peeking in my window!
then I slip on a flimsy nightgown, go outside,
press my face against the glass and wait...

This makes me proud to be an American

where drunk drivers ought to wear necklaces
made from the spines of children they've run over.

I remember my face being invented
through a windshield.

All the wounds stitched with horsehair
So the scars galloped across my forehead.

I remember the hymns cherubs sang
in my bloodstream. The way even my shadow ached
when the chubby infants stopped.

I remember wishing I could be boiled like water
and made pure again. Desire
so real it could be outlined in chalk.

My eyes were the color of palm trees
in a hurricane. I'd wake up
and my id would start the day without me.

Somewhere a junkie fixes the hole in his arm
and a racing car zips around my halo.

A good God is hard to find.

Each morning I look in the mirror
and say *promise me something*
don't do the things I've done.

Friends and High Places

for Mike

It's like escaping a hot, bright room
for the serenity of a city at night, covered in snow.

People eliminated. A carpet of silence
for taxis to whisper across. The world becoming

a pleasant dream of itself. The itch
of want smoldering to life on skin. Memory sends

a chill vanishing between vertebrae.
It's New Year's Eve. *Hail the Calendar!* As if

clocks will pause for a moment
before reloading their long rifles. Years are tiny

freckles on the face of a century.
Where is the constellation we gazed at each night

through a bill rolled so tight
the first President lost his breath, as our eyeballs

literally unraveled? I am alone
in the rectangular borough in the observatory,

where even fire trucks can't rescue
the arsonist stretching his calves in my brain.

Modern Day Sisyphus

I've fallen down the finest steps in Europe.
Mayan temples in Guatemalan jungle.
The ones Rocky conquered.

It made the flags in my head stop burning.
I grew new flags. Truth is

I had trouble sleeping in the real world.

My social life began to revolve around staircases.
Only went to parties in tall buildings. Yeah,

she's whipped cream looking, an alabaster
personality, but what about her stairs?

Got a flat in an eight story walk-up. Landings
so filthy even the rats turned back.

If you see me between flights, clutching a banister,
don't stare. I'm just a shadow of the mood
swinging inside you.

1977

What are they waiting for?

The family around the table and a silence
so compact no words can break it.

Not even a pigeon swirling through the window
can nudge mother's poorly taped grin.

Her face has the euphoric glow of a mathematician
whispering a formula into the whorl of a rose.

Her eyes are tiny stones testing the black
silk bags she lugs them in.

Since father banned television the sons stare
at the marriage dangling from the ceiling.

Each month it sinks another couple inches
until it's in their food.

No wonder they don't eat.

First Person Omniscient

I made her tell me of the affair,
    every detail,
and I became him, the man who pulled
    her into the closet,
opening the many rooms of her mouth,
    knobs spinning,
and then I was her, pulling him
    by the tongue
through the river of rooms in the mansion
    of my mouth,
his eye pressing into me, his eye
    seeing all,
and then I was the closet, the space
    they traveled through
on their way to the mansion, and then the real
    I entered the closet,
the wind of doors slamming, bodies
    rushing, gone—
my eye lost in the mouth of my pocket,
    or is it my hand,
my dirty, awful hand.

The Multiple Floor

Christmas. Again I desert my younger brothers
with freaks disguised as our parents
yanking them back and forth in the snow.

I won't unwrap anyone's expensive feelings for me.
My darkest thoughts dangle from my ears.

An oxygen mask is an abandoned building
neighborhood children learn to breathe in.

A suitcase is what a father carries
down the staircase of broken plates.

I walk through Manhattan, following the footsteps
of God running out on the world.

On Houston Street, a person rattles in a box
like a present so horrible even the wind won't open it.

Glorious and *getting worse* sound the same to me.

Innocence is a finger coming off
in a glove during a snowball fight.

In Tompkins Square, a fiend ties his arm
with Christmas lights and plugs in his only tree.

Panic spreads its hideous cream over the cheeks
of a statue, and I used to be that statue.

I hoist a pale vowel up the throat's pole,
wave it in surrender over the body.

NANCY
MITCHELL

Love Story in Subtitles

Each woman is moved,
one to the slow nursing
of a thin ultra-light cigarette,
one to discreetly blot a tear
from the corner of her eye
with a Kleenex, one to worry
a hangnail on her thumb.

Each feels the story
is her own: love and betrayal
and the accompanying
complications of sex.

They cheer the heroine
when she refuses to compromise
anymore, although they know
from their experiences
in love, it won't be long
before he replaces her.
They are glad
she has taken the dog.

But he gives up
everything to find her again:
his passport, his cushy job
and all the other women
(except for one last fling).
They move to the country and are happy,
make love outdoors and eat dark bread.

When they die in a wrecked car
the women don't even consider
it a tragedy.

They are silent
as the last credits roll
off the screen. One woman
wants to knock out the wall
with a sledgehammer
and let the night in.
The next wants to put her arms
in new plowed earth
all the way up to her elbows.
The other wants to swim
in the black river
that runs through the city—
all night, underwater.

Runaway

You were with us all along,
four blocks from home
in a wooded lot
where men in cherry pickers
unwittingly graced your grave
with dogwood and wisteria
they were cutting clear
from power lines.

Among dazed neighbors I visit
the hole they dug you from.
The shoveled piles of dirt
studded with small red flags
quivering on their wire stems
like tulips out of season.

The moon is stuck flat
to the sky. Walking home
with my daughter I pull her
closer with each car
that passes, cling
to the theory
of the random and drug-crazed,
try not to think
death lives among us
smoking a pipe.

Incognito

In the dream I travel by sea
and arrive in the middle of night.
I'm wet and tremble
from so far a swim.
My dress clings like a silk glove.
I check the effect
in the face of the moon.

I go to your door shivering
and pretend I am shipwrecked.
You ask me to come in,
liking things lost and broken.

You give me your bathrobe,
I wear it. I gently blow
steam from the tea
you bring. You warm my feet
between your hands.
With your tongue you clean
salt from each toe. Still
you don't know it's me.
Still you don't know.

The Leaving

The last night
with him, lying down,
he placed his hand
on the space
where my ribs furl
back like wings.

To steady
me, to keep me
from rising.

MARIE
HOWE

Recovery

You have decided to live. This is your fifth
day living. Hard to sleep. Harder to eat,

the food thick on your tongue, as I watch you,
my own mouth moving.

Is this how they felt after the flood? The floor
a mess, the garden ruined,

the animals insufferable, cooped up so long?
So much work to be done.

The sodden dresses. Houses to be built.
Wood to be dried and driven and stacked. Nails!

The muddy roses. So much muck about. Hard walking.
And still a steady drizzle,

the sun like a morning moon, and all of them grumpy
and looking at each other in that new way.

We walk together, slowly, on this your fifth day
and you, occasionally, glimmer with a light

I've never seen before. It frightens me,
this new muscle in you, flexing.

I had the crutches ready. The soup simmering.
But now it is as we thought.

Can we endure it, the rain finally stopped?

How Many Times

No matter how many times I try I can't stop my father
from walking into my sister's room

and I can't see any better, leaning from here to look
in his eyes. It's dark in the hall

and everyone's sleeping. This is the past
where everything is perfect already and nothing changes,

where the water glass falls to the bathroom floor
and bounces once before breaking.

Nothing. Not the small sound my sister makes, turning
over, not the thump of the dog's tail

when he opens one eye to see him stumbling back to bed
still drunk, a little bewildered.

This is exactly as I knew it would be.
And if I whisper her name, hissing a warning,

I've been doing that for years now, and still the dog
startles and growls until he sees

it's our father, and still the door opens, and she
makes that small *oh* turning over.

The Mother

In her early old age the mother's toenails curl over her toes
so that when she walks across the kitchen floor some click.

The doctor has warned her, for the third time, that her legs will
ulcerate if she doesn't rub moisturizer into them so

unwilling is she to touch her own body or to care for it.
This is the same woman who stood many nights at the foot of the
    attic stairs

as her husband weaved and stammered up into the room where her
    daughter slept
—on the landing, in her bathrobe,

by the laundry chute, unmoving,
like a statue in the children's game her children play—

and now the soft drone of her daughter's waking voice, reasoning and
rising, and the first slap

and the scrape of her son's chair pushed back from his desk,
the air thick now with their separate listening...

and again the girl's voice, now quietly weeping, and the creak of her
    bed...
In the game, someone has to touch you to free you

then you're human again.

The Promise

In the dream I had when he came back, not sick
but whole, and wearing his winter coat,

he looked at me as though he could not speak, as if
there were a law against it, a membrane he couldn't break.

His silence was the thing he could not
not do, like our breathing in this world, like our living,

as we do, in time.
And I told him: *I'm reading all this Buddhist stuff,*

and listen, we don't die. Death is an event,
a threshold we pass through. We go on and on

and into light forever.
And he looked down and then back at me. It was the look we'd pass

across the kitchen table when Dad was drunk again and dangerous,
the level look that wants to tell you something

in a crowded room, something important, and can't.

The Dream

I had a dream in the day:
I laid my father's body down in a narrow boat

and sent him off along the river bank with its cattails and grasses.
And the boat (it was made of skin and wood bent when it was wet.)

took him to his burial finally.
But a day or two later I realized it was my self I wanted

to lay down—hands crossed, eyes closed
—oh, the light coming up from down there,

the sweet smell of the water—and finally, the sense of being carried
by a current I could not name or change.

TESS
GALLAGHER

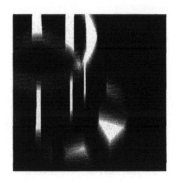

Even Now You Are Leaving

Not to let ourselves know
by a hand held too long, as this last,
words no part of any other, like a mule
trained to carry anything
and not mean it. Just so, these lips
puffed from where you ran into yourself
in a car the night before, the wheel
turning through your mouth
like something you might have said.

I can't believe your face, that
it could fall from here, let alone
my own. Yet prove it, the chin
large now as a forehead. Some nearness
has done this to you, or the lack
of it. That scheme you had
for making us rich, I want to tell you
it worked, though Alaska
stayed due north
and you never touched.

The spar tree axe
swings from a tree you rigged
to hold that clearing. I can't look up.
The tree's too white
and cedar an easy fire. Father,
some neglect is killing us all, but yours
has a name of its own: family,
something gone on without you, your eyes
ruined and terrible in a face
even now you are leaving.

3 A.M. Kitchen: My Father Talking

For years it was land working me, oil fields,
cotton fields, then I got some land. I
worked it. Them days you could just about
make a living. I was logging.

Then I sent to Missouri. Momma
come out. We got married.
We got some kids. Five kids.
That kept us going.

We bought some land near the water.
It was cheap then. The water
was right there. You just looked out
the window. It never left the window.

I bought a boat. Fourteen footer.
There was fish out there then.
You remember, we used to catch
six, eight fish, clean them right
out in the yard. I could of fished to China.

I quit the woods. One day just
walked out, took off my caulks, said that's
it. I went to the docks.
I was driving winch. You had to watch
to see nothing fell out of the sling. If
you killed somebody you'd
never forget it. All
those years I was just working
I was on edge, every day. Just working.

You kids. I could tell you
a lot. But I won't.
It's winter. I play a lot of cards
down at the tavern. Your mother.

I have to think of excuses
to get out of the house. You're
wasting your time, she says. You're wasting
your money.

You don't have no idea, Threasie.
I run out of things
to work for. Hell, why shouldn't I
play cards? Threasie,
some days now I just don't know.

Coming Home

As usual, I was desperate.
I went through your house as if I owned it.
I said, "I need This, This and This."
But contrary to all I know of you,
you did not answer, only looked after me.

I've never seen the house so empty, Mother.
Even the rugs felt it, how little
they covered. And what have you done
with the plants? How thankfully
we thought their green replaced us.

You were keeping something like a light.
I had seen it before, a place you'd never been
or never came back from. It was a special way
your eyes looked out over the water. Whitecaps
lifted the bay and you said, "He should be here
by now."

How he always came back; the drinking,
the fishing into the night, all
the ruthless ships he unloaded.
That was the miracle of our lives. Even now
he won't stay out of what I have
to say to you.

But they worry me, those boxes
of clothes I left in your basement. Sometimes
I think of home as a storehouse, the more
we leave behind, the less
you say. The last time
I couldn't take anything.

So I'm always coming back like tonight,
in a temper, brushing the azaleas

on the doorstep. What did you mean
by it, this tenderness
that is a whip, a longing?

On Your Own

How quickly the postures shift.
Just moments ago we seemed human,
or in the Toledo of my past
I made out I was emotionally illiterate
so as not to feel a pain I deserved.

Here at the Great Southern
some of the boys have made it
into gray suits and pocket calculators.
I'm feeling end-of-season, like a somebody
who's hung around the church
between a series of double weddings.

Friend, what you said about the terror
of American Womanhood,
I forget it already, but I know
what you mean. I'm so scary some days
I'd run from myself. It's hard work
having your way, even
half the time, and having it,
know what not to do with it. Who
hasn't thrown away a life or two
at the mercy of another's passion,
spite or industry.

It's like this on your own: the charms
unlucky, the employment
solitary, the best love always
the benefit of a strenuous doubt.

Kidnaper

He motions me over with a question.
He is lost. I believe him. It seems
he calls my name. I move
closer. He says it again, the name
of someone he loves. I step back pretending

not to hear. I suspect
the street he wants
does not exist, but I am glad to point
away from myself. While he turns
I slip off my wristwatch, already laying a trail
for those who must find me
tumbled like an abandoned car
into the ravine. I lie

without breath for days among ferns.
Pine needles drift
onto my face and breasts
like the tiny hands
of watches. Cars pass.
I imagine it's him
coming back. My death
is not needed. The sun climbs again
for everyone. He lifts me
like a bride

and the leaves fall from my shoulders
in twenty-dollar bills.
"You must have been cold," he says
covering me with his handkerchief.
"You must have given me up."

ETHERIDGE
KNIGHT

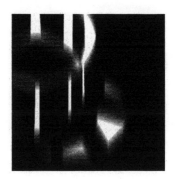

Welcome Back, Mr. Knight: Love of My Life

Welcome back, Mr. K: Love of My Life—
How's your drinking problem?—your thinking
Problem? you / are / pickling
Your liver—
Gotta / watch / out for the
"Ol Liver": Love of My Life.
How's your dope
Problem?—your marijuana, methadone, and cocaine
Problem / too?—your lustful problem—
How's your weight problem—your eating problem?
How's your lying and cheating and
Staying out all / night long problem?
Welcome back, Mr K: Love of My Life
How's your pocket / book problem?—your / being
broke problem? you still owe and borrowing mo'
25 dollar problems from other / po / poets?
Welcome back, Mr. K: Love of My Life.
How's your ex-convict problem?—your John Birch
Problem?—your preacher problem?—your fat
Priests sitting in your / chair, saying
How racist and sexist they / will / forever / be
Problem?—How's your Daniel Moynihan
Problem?—your crime in the streets, runaway
Daddy, Black men with dark shades
And bulging crotches problem?
How's your nixon-agnew—j. edgar hoover
Problem?—you still paranoid? still schizoid?—
Still scared shitless?
How's your bullet-thru-the-brain problem?—or
A needle-in-your-arm problem?
Welcome back, Mr. K:—Love of My Life.
You gotta watch / out for the "Ol Liver."
How's your pussy
Problem?—lady-on-top—
smiling like God, titty-in-your-mouth

Problem? Welcome back, Mr. K:
Love of My Life. How's your peace
Problem?—your no / mo' war
Problem—your heart problem—your belly / problem?—
You gotta watch / out for the "Ol Liver."

Another Poem for Me
(after Recovering from an O.D.)

what now
what now dumb nigger damn near dead
what now
now that you won't dance
behind the pale white doors of death
what now   is   to be
to be what you wanna be
or what white / america wants you to be
a lame crawling from nickel bag to nickel bag
be black brother / man be black
and blooming in the night
be black like your fat brother
sweating and straining to hold you
as you struggle against the straps
be black   be black like
your woman   her painted face floating
above you   her hands sliding
                  under the sheets
to take yours   be black like
your mamma sitting in a quiet corner
praying to a white / jesus to save her black boy

what now dumb nigger damn near dead
where is the correctness
the proper posture
the serious love of living
now that death has fled these quiet corridors

A Wasp Woman Visits a Black Junkie in Prison

After explanations and regulations, he
Walked warily in.
Black hair covered his chin, subscribing to
Villainous ideal.
"This can not be real," he thought, "this is a
Classical mistake;
This is a cake baked with embarrassing icing;
Somebody's got
Likely as not, a big fat tongue in cheek!
What have I to do
With a prim and proper-blooded lady?"
Christ in deed has risen
When a Junkie in prison visits with a Wasp woman.

"Hold your stupid face, man,
Learn a little grace, man; drop a notch the sacred shield.
She might have good reason,
Like: 'I was in prison and ye visited me not,' or—some such.
So sweep clear
Anachronistic fear, fight the fog,
And use no hot words."

After the seating
And the greeting, they fished for a denominator,
Common or uncommon;
And could only summon up the fact that both were human.
"Be at ease, man!
Try to please, man!—the lady is as lost as you:
'You got children, Ma'am?' " he said aloud.
The thrust broke the dam, and their lines wiggled in the water.
She offered no pills
To cure his many ills, no compact sermons, but small
And funny talk:
"My baby began to walk...simply cannot keep his room clean..."
Her chatter sparked no resurrection and truly

No shackles were shaken
But after she had taken her leave, he walked softly,
And for hours used no hot words.

Feeling Fucked Up

Lord she's gone done left me done packed / up and split
and I with no way to make her
come back and everywhere the world is bare
bright bone white   crystal sand glistens
dope death dead dying and jiving drove
her away made her take her laughter and her smiles
and her softness and her midnight sighs—

Fuck Coltrane and music and clouds drifting in the sky
fuck the sea and trees and the sky and birds
and alligators and all the animals that roam the earth
fuck marx and mao fuck fidel and nkrumah and
democracy and communism fuck smack and pot
and red ripe tomatoes fuck joseph fuck mary fuck
god jesus and all the disciples fuck fanon nixon
and malcolm fuck the revolution fuck freedom fuck
the whole muthafucking thing
all I want now is my woman back
so my soul can sing

CINDY
GOFF

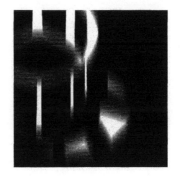

Addiction

I stroll backward through the garden's maze
made of high hedges and sundials
      and commune with gravestones.
I'm learning the language of engravers
whose chisels trick my stubborn spirit
into my hands full of habits
      and I am one of those habits.
I who do not control the teachings of algebra
or the preachings of physics
have unraveled the moon like a moth.
My mouth is full of meteors
that alter my weather daily
and whose dust belongs
behind museum glass
      instead of infecting words.
Soon I will speak through ravens
but first I must gather my bones
and construct an alphabet.
My eyes have nothing to do
but rest on two stone benches
while the sundials point to a shadow
      that's trying to kill me.

I Feel Unattractive during Mating Season

I try impressing you from a barstool
but I keep swaying to one side
because my head is full of shotguns.

The yellow yardstick you keep
between us pokes me in the breast
and a herd of cattle, who normally reside there,
walk to my groin. Their cowbells and moos
vibrate between my legs.

I reveal to you that I paint
windows in my house black to prevent crimes.

But you keep smiling at a long-legged gazelle
loudly doing her nails in your blind spot.

I spin a Lewis Carroll book on my finger
while reciting medieval poetry backward.

She says, "Hi."

A shotgun fires in my head
bullets eject through my temple
and shatter a shelf full of beer mugs.

The bartender buys me a drink.

I watch you stroke
her striped fur
and gently pull her head down by her horn
so you can whisper something in her ear.

Drinking Beer with Sir

My legs fell asleep in an attempt
not to rub against his knees.
As he chatted, I was afraid he knew

I was counting the number of times
we had embraced.
I meditated on these numbers
while sitting on the barstool.
I have never been so intimate with calculations.

When my gestures nearly touched him,
he cleared his throat,
and I cowardly traced a limb on the table.
I thought if I touched his face,
he would turn into blue smoke
curling around my fingers.

I reached out to feel
his shoulder. My hand
went through him and broke a bottle.

He took me home
and pulled glass out of my fingers
without touching me.

Turning into an Oak Tree

I look down at my husband leaving me.
I'm seventy feet taller than he is now.
The bones in my arms splinter into thousands of twigs;
my legs grow together and twist
into the ground. It doesn't matter
where my car is parked or where my house keys have fallen;
I no longer care what I weigh.
I am sturdier than a hundred men.
From up here I can see Cape Cod,
shaped like a lobster tail.
I watch my husband become a speck
and consider how I'll miss
being touched.

The First Sober Morning

No one is awake in the campgrounds
of the dismantled carnival. The hermaphrodite sleeps
with the levers of her roller coaster.
The nymphomaniac is curled up in a Ferris wheel seat.
The fat lady sleeps sitting up in front of a carousel mirror.
And the young college student, who just wanted to earn money
for Europe, is middle-aged now. She snores on a straw bed
in the geek pit.
I'm so afraid of telling them
we will not be moving to a new town.

LYNDA
HULL

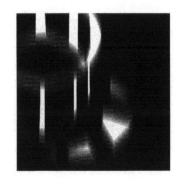

Adagio

Across Majestic Boulevard, *Steam Bath*
neons the snow to blue, and on her table
a blue cup steams, a rime of stale cream
circling its rim. Before finding the chipped case

behind the mirror, she waits for morning
the way an addict must wait, a little longer,
and studies the torn print on the wall—
lilies blurred to water stains, a woman

floating in a boat trailing fingers
in its wake. Someone rich. Someone gone.
Maybe a countess. She lets herself drift in the boat
warming thin translucent hands in coffee steam.

She's not a countess, only another girl
from the outer boroughs with a heroin habit as long
as the sea routes that run up and down the coast.
She's read all winter a life of Hart Crane, losing

her place, beginning again with Crane in a room
by the bridge, the East River, spending himself
lavishly. She's spent her night
circulating between piano bars and cabarets

where Greek sailors drink and buy her
cheap hotel champagne at 10 bucks a shot
before evaporating to another port on the map
of terra incognita the waterlilies chart

along her wall. The mantel is greened with
a chemical patina of sweat and time, and she can't
call any of this back. Hart Crane sways,
a bottle of scotch in one hand, his face plunged

inside the gramophone's tin trumpet, jazzed
to graceless oblivion. She rinses her face
in the basin, cold water, then turns to glance
across the boulevard where life's arranged

in all its grainy splendor. The steam bath sign
switches off with dawn, a few departing men
swathed in pea coats. The bath attendant climbs
as always to the roof, then opens the dovecote

to let his pigeons fly before descending to his berth.
They bank and curve towards the harbor that surrenders
to the sea. She knows Crane will leap
from the *Orizaba*'s stern to black fathoms

of water, that one day she'll lock this room
and lose the key. The gas flame's yellow coronet
stutters and she rolls her stocking down at last
to hit the vein above her ankle, until carried forward

she thinks it's nothing but the velocity of the world
plunging through space, the tarnished mirror
slanted on the mantel showing a dove-gray sky
beginning to lighten, strangely, from within.

Visiting Hour

From the hospital solarium we watch row houses
change with evening down the avenue, the gardener

bending to red asters, his blond chrysanthemums.
Each day I learn more of the miraculous.

The gardener rocks on his heels and softly
Riva talks to me about the d.t.'s, her gin

hallucinations. The willow on the lawn
is bare, almost flagrant in the wind off

Baltimore harbor. She wants me to brush her hair.
Some mornings I'd hear her sing to herself

numbers she knew by heart
from nightclubs on the waterfront circuit.

I wondered if she watched herself dissolve
in the mirror as shadows flickered, then whispering

gathered. Floating up the airshaft
her hoarse contralto broke over "I Should Care,"

"Unforgettable," and in that voice
everything she remembered—the passage

from man to man, a sequence of hands
undressing her, letting her fall like the falling

syllables of rain she loves, of steam, those trains
and ships that leave. How she thought for years

a departure or a touch might console her, if only
for the time it takes luck to change, to drink

past memory of each stranger that faltered
over her body until her song was a current

of murmurs that drew her into sleep, into
the shapes of her fear. Insects boiling

from the drain, she tells me, a plague
of veiled nuns. Her hair snaps, electric

in the brush, long, the color of dust or rain
against a gunmetal sky. I saw her once, at the end

of a sullen July dusk so humid that the boys
loitering outside the Palace Bar & Grill

moved as if through vapor. She was reeling
in spike heels, her faded blue kimono.

They heckled her and showered her with pennies,
spent movie tickets. But she was singing.

That night I turned away and cursed myself
for turning. She holds a glass of water

to show her hands have grown more steady.
Look, she whispers, and I brush

and braid and the voices of visiting hour rise
then wind like gauze. The gardener's flowers nod,

pale in the arc lamps that rinse the factory boys
shooting craps as they always do down on

Sweet Air Avenue. I know they steam the dice
with breath for luck before they toss,

and over them the air shimmers the way still water
shimmers as gulls unfold like Riva's evening hands

across the sky, tremulous, endangered.

Lost Fugue for Chet

Chet Baker, Amsterdam, 1988

A single spot slides the trumpet's flare then stops
   at that face, the extraordinary ruins thumb-marked
with the hollows of heroin, the rest chiaroscuroed.
   Amsterdam, the final gig, canals & countless

stone bridges arc, glimmered in lamps. Later this week
   his Badlands face, handsome in a print from thirty
years ago, will follow me from the obituary page
   insistent as windblown papers by the black cathedral

of St. Nicholas standing closed today: pigeon shit
   & feathers, posters swathing tarnished doors, a litter
of syringes. Junkies cloud the gutted railway station blocks
   & dealers from doorways call *coca, heroina,* some throaty

foaming harmony. A measured inhalation, again
   the sweet embouchure, metallic, wet stem. Ghostly,
the horn's improvisations purl & murmur
   the narrow *strasses* of *Rosse Buurt,* the district rife

with purse-snatchers, women alluring, desolate, poised
   in blue windows, Michelangelo boys, hair spilling
fluent running chords, mares' tails in the sky green
   & violet. So easy to get lost, these cavernous

brown cafés. Amsterdam, & its spectral fogs, its
   bars & softly shifting tugboats. He builds once more
the dense harmonic structure, the gabled houses.
   Let's get lost. Why court the brink & then step back?

After surviving, what arrives? So what's the point
   when there are so many women, creamy callas with single
furled petals turning in & in upon themselves
   like variations, nights when the horn's coming

genius riffs, metal & spit, that rich consuming rush
   of good dope, a brief languor burnishing
the groin, better than any sex. Fuck Death.
   In the audience, there's always this gaunt man, cigarette

in hand, black Maserati at the curb, waiting,
   the fast ride through mountain passes, descending with
no rails between asphalt & precipice. Inside, magnetic
   whispering *take me there, take me.* April, the lindens

& horse chestnuts flowering, cold white blossoms
   on the canal. He's lost as he hears those inner voicings,
a slurred veneer of chords, molten, fingering
   articulate. His glance below Dutch headlines, the fall

"accidental" from a hotel sill. Too loaded. What do you do
   at the brink? Stepping back in time, I can only
imagine the last hit, lilies insinuating themselves
   up your arms, leaves around your face, one hand vanishing

sabled to shadow. The newsprint photo & I'm trying
   to recall names, songs, the sinuous figures, but facts
don't matter, what counts is out of pained dissonance,
   the sick vivid green of backstage bathrooms, out of

broken rhythms—and I've never forgotten, never—
   this is the tied-off vein, this is 3 A.M. terror
thrumming, this is the carnation of blood clouding
   the syringe, you shaped *summer rains across the quays*

of Paris, flame suffusing jade against a girl's
   dark ear. From the trumpet, pawned, redeemed, pawned again
you formed one wrenching blue arrangement, a phrase endlessly
   complicated as that twilit dive through smoke, applause,

the pale haunted rooms. Cold chestnuts flowering April
   & you're falling from heaven in a shower of eighth notes
to the cobbled street below & foaming dappled horses
   plunge beneath the still green waters of the Grand Canal.

DENIS
JOHNSON

The Heavens

From mind to mind
I am acquainted with the struggles
of these stars. The very same
chemistry wages itself minutely
in my person.
It is all one intolerable war.
I don't care if we're fugitives,
we are ceaselessly exalted, rising
like the drowned out of our shirts...

The Honor

At a party in a Spanish kind of tiled house
I met a woman who had won an award
for writing whose second prize
had gone to me. For years
I'd felt a kinship with her in the sharing
of this honor,
and I told her how glad I was to talk with her,
my compatriot of letters,
mentioning of course this award.
But it was nothing
to her, and in fact she didn't remember it.
I didn't know what else to talk about.
I looked around us at a room full of hands
moving drinks in tiny, rapid circles—
you know how people do
with their drinks.

Soon after this I became
another person, somebody
I would have brushed off if I'd met him that night,
somebody I never imagined.

People will tell you that it's awful
to see facts eat our dreams, our presumptions,
but they're wrong. It is an honor
to learn to replace one hope with another.
It was the only thing that could possibly have persuaded me
that my life is not a lonely story played out
in barrooms before a vast audience of the dead.

The Words of a Toast

The man wants to make love to the crippled man's sister
because he loves the crippled man.
The man cries
beside the bed of the man who cannot breathe.

He stands in the parking lot, turning in the sun.
He says to the restaurant, I'm closed,
and to the sunlight, Why don't you arrest me?

But the spring changes so thickly among the buildings, the sun
brightens so sharply on the walls,
and the air tastes so sweetly of the rightness of things—
suddenly thinking of his crippled friend: Oh, God,

you wanted water,
didn't you? and you with only tears for a voice.
What can I do now?
What can I do for you but drink this glass of water?

CINDY DAY
ROBERTS

The Leopard

*...when delights spring out of our depths like leopards
our soul's life is in danger.*

—Thomas Merton

The leopard seemed harmless
when he was sleeping.
All I want now is peace
you said so many times.

Amen, I said, I've had it
with running around.
I was wearing my straw hat
with the cherries on it,

you smoked your meerschaum,
I drank my Côtes du Rhône,
you liked your vocabulary
and altogether delighted

we walked around Green Lake
calling out the flowers' names.
After about six months
of this we bought the house.

Next we sat on the patio
in the new lawn chairs
and admired the sun setting
over Syracuse, called it peace.

But the leopard was stretched
out beside us. He licked
himself clean beside us,
dozed and his content

rumbled in his chest.
He had fed lately on

passion and could wait.
He knew it would come again,

the desperation, and we,
having moved as usual
a little too fast, feeling
ourselves safe, god-like,

when we were only the same
two cranks in fancy clothes,
kept him as an exotic
pet, something wild

that would sleep on the patio.
To make a long story short
the leopard tore us to pieces,
ate us up. But you know that

and about all the regret.
The real story comes after,
the one about the soul.
Anyone can have a leopard.

Poor Zelda

As far as the poem was concerned
it would not let her in. It was

just too hard for her. It did not
want her but itself through her

and this Zelda dancing to
her image in the antique mirror

could not give. That is why we call her,
Poor, half-humorously. For she

took on so fantastically the great
dilemma: how to die to oneself

to live free. First, if you remember,
she took on Scott (now there

was a job) in love; became
his character—a muse, and then

a drunk. Or did he take on her?
It was confused, that kind of love

and soon together they attacked
headwaiters. Thus having reached

a real despair she tried the poem.
She was going to be a ballerina,

a novelist, finally a painter.
She bought an enormous mirror

in Philadelphia, had it brought
to their last mansion, the one

with the beautiful name, Ellerslie,
and practised her leaps and bends until

the muscles in her legs distorted
and Scott said he would go mad.

It is funny, it is funny, and yet
I think of her so tenderly and of

the poem's cruelty. She wanted it
for herself, to save, in the end,

her life, to hide in, to be with,
to say all that pain. And of course

it would not let her in. It barely
let in Scott, I don't know why,

that would make another poem,
that story. Zelda it destroyed.

I don't know why. She was perhaps
a little more selfish than he was;

more arrogant. The line wouldn't
hold her. It just wouldn't. Broke.

Enough

A moon the color of an empty movie screen
lit up the orchard. We could see
the individual apples; we could see
our faces. Everything in empty light
visible yet gray, mysterious.

Wherever I go I am trying to learn my story.
The story of my life. On this night
I walked with Mary and Kevin and their child,
Nora, into the orchard. A harvest moon walk,
Mary called it. Nora danced in the clearing.

It was partly a story of forgiveness.
One summer I abandoned my child
and they took her in. They forgave me
and I forgave them for being what I was not.

It was also a story of being alone
among friends. Several times
we stopped to look up at the moon,
its light on the pond, on the
tall grass. I tilted my head back
to see the sky, the sky on my face
and my separateness from these things
even as I stood among them.

But then too, it was a story of wanting to be
a part of the world just by walking out into it.

It was a story about the story Nora told
in her tiny voice by the side of the pond;
a ghost story, she told us, about a girl
who tied a green ribbon in her hair
and then her head fell off.
In one way Nora was the closest one

to the moon. In another
she was already putting fiction
between herself and living.

It was a story the night told:
I am enough just as I am—that
is what the eternal sky said.
And the man, woman and child—
we are all enough.

Let Go of It

When the wind came up that day
I was holding the jib, I was holding it tight
like Harriet said to and it was something
to be flying over the bright water,
the wind with us, the shore becoming small,
then green, then a dark line.

It was my first time and I was glad
that it was easy, my job steady,
the boat light as a toy, the water
slipping by with a slipping sound.

And then the wind changed, turning
like a face in anger, darkly,
and hurled itself at the side of us.
Harriet said, "Let go of it," but I couldn't,
I kept pulling the jib tighter while the mainsail
she let go of clapped over my head
and the rope tying everything to everything
dug deep into my hands. Disaster is
to me now this perfect symbol,
that boat keeling, Harriet leaning backward
over starboard, arching her neck as far as it will go
into the wind, the volume of the wind,
the Atlantic spilling in, again
her cry, "Let go of it!" and myself
when I couldn't, when it was more than
terror, I already believed I was stronger,
bigger than the wind and could not see
how not holding on would save us,
how letting go is holding on.

WILLIAM LORAN
SMITH

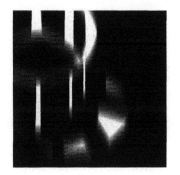

The Family Man

There are men so crazy from not having something,
that they build temples to it, and walk under the groins
and spires, chanting to the emptiness of it, and when night
unrolls its mattress for their pallet, they put a picture
of it on the table, and lie down pretending it has come
to keep them warm in its green sparkling dress,
with the mink head on the shoulder, curling back its vicious lip.

There are men so crazy from not having something,
that they dress their daughters in blue skirts and white tights,
and take them to the circus where the children squeal
at the clowns bumping and tumbling in their eyes.
So crazy, they promise their daughters white plumed horses,
and cotton candy, and pinwheels of happiness forever.
And then these crazy men go home, and while the house
is four ticks of their antique clocks, and two winter breaths,
they close the garage door, lie down on the front seats
of their Chevys and let the engine sing its sweet song.

There are men so crazy from not having something,
they drive to a bar in Albuquerque, and laugh
at the lewd cartoon napkins of big-chested women
leaning over just so. They sit there for years
until She sidles up and, claiming to have it, bends
her legs back, and lets him taste the juicy red eye of it.
There are men so crazy that George Jones is their hero,
and while *"He stopped loving her today"* plays on the radio,
they wash down the pills from the silver turquoise locket,
and see God's blue face, blank and pure above the buttes.

There are men so crazy from not having something,
they marry prom queens at the Love Forever chapel,
and then for twenty years slap their silly faces for looking
at them while they eat, and the kids listen through
the ears of the honey-yellow walls to their father's voice

making their mother a tiny, dried-up flower, all light
and shed of skin when she comes to kiss them in the dark.

There are men so crazy from not having something,
that they become women and stick their fingers into
the wet, dark, cave of themselves to feel the ribs
of where they were pulled out by the stainless steel tongs
and wrapped in cotton receiving blankets, and taught
by the nurse to take the rubber nipple without choking.
So crazy like this, that they smell the kinky black hair
under a woman's arms, and become insane with a memory
like a hand thrusting up and up again through the icy water.

There are men so crazy from not having something,
that in one day, nothing and everything is it.
The wafer of moon burning in their foreheads is it,
and the Uncle Sam in his red and white rags waving
a novelty flag at all the cars on Fourth Street,
and wives who give it away they have so much of it,
even the slobbering smiles of their black dogs are it.

There are men so crazy from not having something,
that their bones are it, and the muscles of their hearts
are it. The eyes, the night, all of the night and the path.
The light and Christ are it. The cells flying off their fat
bodies are it. The gallery of suits, the needle's last rites,
the governor playing golf and the phone not ringing are it.
The crow engulfing its own huge shadow,
the grass, the insects, the wars, the missile biting
into the children's ward. Everything is crazy with it.
Wanting it, dreaming it, sucking it, needing it,
Until all the tunnels and the ends of the earth are it.

A Good Man's Fate

At a quarter of five in the morning a sparrow worries
the mulch underneath the porch light, as my father
lights a cigarette and stands by the Dutch door in the kitchen
watching the pale eye of moon fade away.
In his half-eaten brain, the first flame of vodka moves
with only potential through the ruins of his simple wishes,
and he is sure God's voice is a thousand birds singing
between this dark and light. He is sure that his wife
will call him to her bed, where he will finally press himself
against her back, his perfect cock nestled between her legs.
Her nipples hard from the spit he has licked onto his fingers.

At a quarter of five in the morning my father
is the saint of emptiness, he washes clean all the world's
trouble in that first swig. There is so much to believe in,
that his gut burns with the pain of not loving it enough.
And he knows full well how hearses purr and wind their way
down the manicured hills, and how many tons of dirt
it takes to cover the whirling polished atoms of a cherry casket.

My father is a visionary, he can see his pores bleed
their grayness before our very eyes. How soon, his grandson
will wait all day for him to rise and take him down by the river
to watch the tugboats go churning by. You were great, Father,
how you divined those waters of the dead, the way you held
the quivering willow branch over your soiled sheets,
over the mumbling of our names, over the thick
muscled arms of the nun who prayed by your bed.
The way you fulfilled all your prophecies like a king.

Butchertown

The fine brick houses are crumbling,
falling after a hundred years of widows
skimming tallow off the creek, and teams
of Morgans whipped up these roads.
He told me today on the bus,
about the four thousand a day they kill,
how he knocks the horns clean off
when they stumble down the chutes.
He takes a swig of beer and shows me,
his huge black arms heavy with the hollow
crash against the back of my metal seat.

And I am flung against the railing blocks away,
wondering what he can tell his wife,
how much she can understand, when he comes
home at night, drunk like this, hands still warm
from the friction of steel, the rip of saws.
Wondering, if he wakes in the middle of the night,
and sees a line reaching from her belly to breast.
We are so far over the edge here,
that I feel the brush of wings, taste the blood
of wounded angels borne on simple pallets
through the town. I am the rat's eye in the hay.
And in those seconds after he swings,
my eyes roll back, and I can only ring the bell,
walk down the aisle, this part of me gone.

Sole of Dover

On my parents' honeymoon, my mother stood not
ten feet away from the one and only Frank Sinatra,
who was swaying at the blackjack table, dead drunk
and pissed at being ten thousand down, pissed
at this little shit who's been betting against him
all night, making snide comments behind his back.
So when he says something really sick about Frank's wife,
he turns and lays the guy out on the plush casino carpet.
Blood everywhere and all the people slapping Frank
on the back. All this happening, when my mother
has one of those epiphanies that hit you right
in the stomach, and she knows she will never love
my father who's back in the room sleeping off three
whiskey sours and a porterhouse steak. She thinks,
I shine and that will be enough, some fly boy will come
and take me, part my fine white flesh, flake me off
in tender forkfuls. Thought she was the sole of Dover,
my mother did, as Frank brushed by her, letting his
hand rest for just a second on her hip.

Two days later when they're driving through the desert,
they hear on the radio about this small time hood
who's found in the trunk of a late model Ford,
parked out back of the Sands hotel. My father tries
to describe how they always make a rookie pry it open,
this comic rite of passage when his head snaps back.
But my mother feels like puking, never really puts two
and two together. She thinks Frank shines and that will
be enough, that he will come and take her to that small
town park. And all the little boys will stop and look
while the football floats through the twilight sky.
Then later the moon will stream down through the slates

of a gazebo, burning into his tan muscular shoulders.
She thought I shine and that will be enough.
How the satin makes them quiver and the stars come
out at night. Thought she was the sole of Dover, my mother did.

MICHAEL
BURKARD

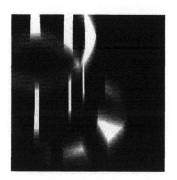

Your Sister Life

Mr. Nobody stood in his doorway—
no one there in that night.

Another night, who knows?—someone
like your old sister might be stopping
in the dark to knock and knock,

until you tell her
"no."

"No"—a sound like the wind
if you want it to be...

just say so,
try it.

If you're thinking of her now
it's raining, and she's asleep,
in some little town

you haven't found yet.
No. You found the place years ago,

you were there.
They said so, you agreed.

You left
to see

if you could know her from afar.
And a town, a star.
A sentimental reason

to say "no one."
Your sister life will find a way
of supporting just about any

of your own conclusions.
Stopping in the dark
to knock and knock.

She's there.
You don't have to let her in.

Woman in the Red House

I did not want to kiss the famous writer.
She was standing close to the table.
I got up and kissed her on the cheek.
I felt like a fool.
I stood, almost toe to toe, and cramped by my chair.
We didn't exchange a word, she continued talking with her friend,
and I sat down.

This is what I am like.
I am like this also: I believe in the rain which continues,
I believe the clock on the wall is a clock on the wall, although
whatever this function of time is I am not so sure.
Once I believed in lies, now I believe in the sun.
And the hissing of a dream which is famous.

I also believe it is not very important what I believe,
at least not to you,
or the man on the stairs,
or the man on the train.
The woman in the red house may consider my belief important
— I will be sure of that only when the system of rage
perishes within me.

If this rage does not perish I wish to.

I bought the famous writer's book today.
I will read it, then give it as a gift.
Unsuspecting gift, unsuspecting train.
Voyage of a fool through the life.

Sober Ghost

My mother, Nettie, and her sister, Lelia,
heard, as children, the ghost of their Aunt Anna's feet
shuffling across the upstairs floors.
Upon a timid and frightened inspection
they would, of course, find no one.
Lela insists they heard Anna's bedroom window close
—my mother never agreed.

I never walked with either mother or Aunt Lelia under the stars at night.
Anna I pretended walked with me, through the grass, across the white
    river
which flows a few hundred yards behind the apple trees.
This was my version of walking with the dead. I talked to her,
she never talked back.
Only a few years into my drinking I began to hear voices—one was
    Anna's.
Her voice spoke directly behind my eyes. It was a quiet voice,
it was as if I was simply overhearing her.

I never thought it unnatural that I heard her voice, or Roethke's voice,
the other voice I heard. There is a photograph of the American poet
    Roethke
on the cover of his *Collected Poems.* His hair is white against a blue
    background.
I was almost more enthralled by the photograph
than by his poems, and I would hear his voice. This voice
felt more like the possessed, and soon
I felt more like the possessed for hearing it.
A few years later I tore the jacket/photo because of this feeling of
being possessed.

When I tore Roethke I must have torn Anna's voice—
sober or intoxicated, I heard neither voice again.
A decade later I traded my copy of *The Cantos*
for the jacket/photo of Roethke. I traded with a drinking friend.

We laughed: *The Cantos* had been a gift to me from the mother of a man who used me.

Even on that day I did not tell my friend or anyone of the voices, and even having Roethke's white face again did not bring back his voice or Anna's voice. And no amount of drinking or drinking less brought them back either.

Perhaps by tearing his face apart I had broken their spell. It did not break the spell of drinking, but then I did not want to break the drinking spell.

Even recurring dreams can break if you tell someone the dream. I finally wrote a recurring dream once and that killed it. But like the voices I then missed the dream.

Sometimes someone tells me of a recluse writer or painter, and she or he is still drinking somewhere, or he or she is known to be out there in a specific place but so reclusive that it doesn't matter, whereabouts "unknown." And being an alcoholic, even in recovery, I have this more than momentary sense that dark life isn't so bad after all. There is an alcoholic shine to that darkness. It's enough of a longing to make me tremble. And then I turn back, as I do here.

The Summer after Last

I do not want to belabor invisibility,
but if it isn't there in the spaces
among the people as a spiritual thread
then I do not want to be there either.

Sea or no sea, house or not.

There is a useless rage in returning
to the past. It is a labor
not unlike labor among the stones,
5 years time and someone is made to break them
for nothing.

Sea or no sea, house or not.

In the unrational time of the summer
after last I found myself alone
with the sun, simple night,
water when I wanted water.
My heart almost broke for not
being used to this.

It is amazing, the chains attempted
upon the heart.

Sea or no sea, house or not.

How I Shaded the Book

I was in the town before my end. I knew more deeply
than before I was in trouble with drinking.
I received a copy of a Graham Greene novel, *The End of the Affair,* in
    the mail.
I sat down to read it one night, sure I would not like it,
but I could not stop reading.
I felt the romance of the book was validating one more wild
    prolonged fling,
alcohol at the center of the fling. I had no one in mind but I knew
    there would be
someone. And I knew it would be trouble.
The novel made me feel as if I could see it all.

In the middle of the night there was a knock on the door.
A neighbor—I had met no one in the few days I had been in town—
asked if I would drive her and her daughter to the hospital.
Her daughter was sick, she had no car. She had seen my light.
For some reason I was glad to do so. I took the book.
The wait was long, the mother finally told me I could leave,
she could call a relative if they had to leave the hospital.

I saw them on the street days later—she hardly spoke—I wondered if
    it was because
we were of different races. She simply nodded when I asked if her daughter
was all right.
They left their house within a month. The house became a place for
    itinerants.
Six families in six months. One afternoon I heard screaming and cackling
and looked out the window to see an overweight man who could
    hardly walk
limping and tilting away from the old woman on the porch.
She both screamed and cackled. The overweight man finally
hobbled off like an old wagon.

I want to thank the woman and her child for interrupting my reverie.
Although I proceeded to wildly continue an affair for drinking
I feel that couple as a pull from life, a pull
from a source I was for a final time denying.
The book meant more than life. How I shaded the book
meant more than anything, anyone.

But Beautiful

But beautiful is the dog lost,
once headed east, then later

in the dark south. But
beautiful is the cold

which never seems to stay.
Dead Robert is but beautiful,

although other than that
I know not what to say.

Never knew him. Only
in stories told to me

by Charlie does the sun
shine on Robert. And Martha

is but beautiful, though
always was the sense we

conversed in small circles,
nevertheless conversed.

And another Charlie and
another Martha, two old

cousins gone now who-
knows-where. But they

were fine, had a big
old honestly red barn

and a dog whose name
I forget who one Sunday

was attacked by a por-
cupine. But beautiful

is Jane, and Jay and
Clay. Jane is ill,

too ill to be known
for the time being.

But beautiful, like
a simple star shining

when the day is still
dying, and night

wonders if it can
get up, and out.

But beautiful is
the beginning, the

day dear, near or far.
Simple people.

Some who die, some
who die while in

your life. Some who
do violent things.

Some who are forgiven
by themselves. But

beautiful is the drive
up the river's side.

All these people
have taken it.

Like a fairy tale
in which the hero

or heroine, son
or daughter, receives

a song of grace,
a secret grace, to

bestow upon the
journey when the time

arrives. But
beautiful to retrieve

them, one by one,
and one for all.

JEAN
VALENTINE

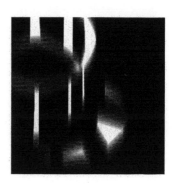

The Summer Was Not Long Enough

Stanley, my ex, the painter,
stepped out of his van.
His beard was gone. Loudly, carefully,
he started to paint the trees
and the ground and the telephone poles
grass green.

Funny, I was crying
after him: not Stan's upsidedown-ness,
my own. My own friends, not written back,
not called. Oh our love
turned from, and August half over.

August's more than half over;
Dove, it's time for peace.
Time to taste the round mountains, the white and green,
and the dusk rose of relationship, again,
for the first time, it's time to take off our clothes,
and the fortresses around our eyes, to touch our first fingers,
you and I, like God, across everything.

American River Sky Alcohol Father

What is pornography? What is dream?
American River Sky Alcohol Father,
forty years ago, four lifetimes ago,
brown as bourbon, warm, you said to me,
"Sorry sorry sorry sorry sorry."
Then: "You're killing your mother."
And she: "You're killing your father."
What do men want? What do fathers want?
Why won't they go to the mothers?
(What do the mothers want.)
American River Sky Alcohol Father,
your warm hand. Your glass. Your bedside table gun.
The dock, the water, the fragile, tough beach grass.
Your hand. I wouldn't swim. I wouldn't fly.

Everyone Was Drunk

South Dakota, August 1989. The buffaloes' deep red-brown
hinged shoulders and beards, their old hinged humps...
These are the old males, separated from the herd.
You can get a state license to shoot them.

"So who saved me? And for what purpose?"

The rich WASP suburb, 1946. The fight
about the Jews on Wall Street. My uncle said,
I thought that's what we fought the war about.
My uncle was right; everyone was drunk; my mother
was peeling shivers of Scotch tape off the counter, peeling off
her good hope. Or was it I who was losing my hope? in the
violent lightning white on the white lawn.
So why was I handed out of the burning window?
For joy. Journalism. Stories.

The Drinker's Wife Writes Back

(A suburb, 1947)

You never hear me, your letter said.
But I was the one who always listened
and understood, reliable, listening
at your thought's door...I was steady
as the oak our bed is made of...

The name of a good doctor, your letter said.
I wait in his green waiting room;
my hands are big, pale, idle. Neutral, intent,
his secretary calls me 'Dear,'
like one of my own children.

He is kind. I can't last out the hour.
The window panes behind him stare me down,
the lenses over his eyes. He asks, What brings me here?
But I feel—not naked—
but absent, made of air

because how could I ever have told
anyone how it was, how the lighted house
went out in the gin brightness
you called 'the war'—and that I did this to you—
I did not do this...

Night Lake

He must have been one or two, I was five,
my brother Johnny's cock
floated like a rose of soap in the tub;
it had the faint, light rock of the boat
you carry in you when you're on land again
at the end of the day...

Oh all I've never gotten written down!
On paper, on my skin. Oh navy blue lake
that I want to drink
to the bottom. And you,
Barrie, what can I give you to drink?
Not the flask of ourselves, we already have that.

The solitude drink
in the kerosene lamplight at the caravan table...

Forces

This man, blind and honored,
listens to his student reader;
this man did what he thought he should do
and sickens in jail; another
comes to the end of his work;
another threw himself out.

Us too, our destinies get on,
into middle age.

Today we visited a field of graves—
slaves' or Indians' graves, you said—
sunk, unmarked, green edges of hammered granite
sharp as a shoulder blade.
      God break me out
of this stiff life I've made.

Trust Me

Who did I write last night? leaning
over this yellow pad, here, inside,
making blue chicken tracks: two
sets of blue footprints, tracking out
on a yellow ground,
child's colors.

Who am I?
who want so much to move
like a fish through water,
through life...
                    Fish *like* to be
underwater.

Fish move through fish! Who
are you?

And Trust Me said, There's another way to go,
we'll go by the river which is frozen under the snow;

my shining, your shining life draws close, draws closer,
God fills us as a woman fills a pitcher.

The River at Wolf

Coming east we left the animals
pelican beaver osprey muskrat and snake
their hair and skin and feathers
their eyes in the dark: red and green.
Your finger drawing my mouth.

Blessed are they who remember
that what they now have they once longed for.

A day a year ago last summer
God filled me with himself, like gold, inside,
deeper inside than marrow.

This close to God this close to you:
walking into the river at Wolf with
the animals. The snake's
green skin, lit from inside. Our second life.

RAYMOND
CARVER

Alcohol

That painting next to the brocaded drapery
is a Delacroix. This is called a divan
not a davenport: this item is a settee.
Notice the ornate legs.
Put on your tarboosh. Smell the burnt cork
under your eyes. Adjust your tunic, so.
Now the red cummerbund and Paris; April 1934.
A black Citröen waits at the curb.
The street lamps are lit.
Give the driver the address, but tell him
not to hurry, that you have all night.
When you get there, drink, make love,
do the shimmy and the beguine.
And when the sun comes up over the Quarter
next morning and that pretty woman
you've had and had all night
now wants to go home with you,
be tender with her, don't do anything
you'll be sorry for later. Bring her home
with you in the Citröen, let her sleep
in a proper bed. Let her
fall in love with you and you
with her and then…something: alcohol,
a problem with alcohol, always alcohol—
what you've really done
and to someone else, the one
you meant to love from the start.

It's afternoon, August, sun striking
the hood of a dusty Ford
parked on your driveway in San Jose.
In the front seat a woman
who is covering her eyes and listening
to an old song on the radio.
You stand in the doorway and watch.

You hear the song. And it is long ago.
You look for it with the sun in your face.
But you don't remember.
You honestly don't remember.

NyQuil

Call it iron discipline. But for months
I never took my first drink
before eleven P.M. Not so bad,
considering. This was in the beginning
phase of things. I knew a man
whose drink of choice was Listerine.
He was coming down off Scotch.
He bought Listerine by the case,
and drank it by the case. The back seat
of his car was piled high with dead soldiers.
Those empty bottles of Listerine
gleaming in his scalding back seat!
The sight of it sent me home soul-searching.
I did that once or twice. Everybody does.
Go way down inside and look around.
I spent hours there, but
didn't meet anyone, or see anything
of interest. I came back to the here and now,
and put on my slippers. Fixed
myself a nice glass of NyQuil.
Dragged a chair over to the window.
Where I watched a pale moon struggle to rise
over Cupertino, California.
I waited through hours of darkness with NyQuil.
And then, sweet Jesus! the first sliver
of light.

Drinking While Driving

It's August and I have not
read a book in six months
except something called *The Retreat From Moscow*
by Caulaincourt.
Nevertheless, I am happy
riding in a car with my brother
and drinking from a pint of Old Crow.
We do not have any place in mind to go,
we are just driving.
If I closed my eyes for a minute
I would be lost, yet
I could gladly lie down and sleep forever
beside this road.
My brother nudges me.
Any minute now, something will happen.

Luck

I was nine years old.
I had been around liquor
all my life. My friends
drank too, but they could handle it.
We'd take cigarettes, beer,
a couple of girls
and go out to the fort.
We'd act silly.
Sometimes you'd pretend
to pass out so the girls
could examine you.
They'd put their hands
down your pants while
you lay there trying
not to laugh, or else
they would lean back,
close their eyes, and
let you feel them all over.
Once at a party my dad
came to the back porch
to take a leak.
We could hear voices
over the record player,
see people standing around
laughing and drinking.
When my dad finished
he zipped up, stared a while
at the starry sky—it was
always starry then
on summer nights—
and went back inside.
The girls had to go home.
I slept all night in the fort
with my best friend.
We kissed on the lips

and touched each other.
I saw the stars fade
toward morning.
I saw a woman sleeping
on our lawn.
I looked up her dress,
then I had a beer
and a cigarette.
Friends, I thought this
was living.
Indoors, someone
had put out a cigarette
in a jar of mustard.
I had a straight shot
from the bottle, then
a drink of warm collins mix,
then another whisky.
And though I went from room
to room, no one was home.
What luck, I thought.
Years later,
I still wanted to give up
friends, love, starry skies,
for a house where no one
was home, no one coming back,
and all I could drink.

The Old Days

You'd dozed in front of the TV
but you hadn't been to bed yet
when you called. I was asleep,
or nearly, when the phone rang.
You wanted to tell me you'd thrown
a party. And I was missed.
It was like the old days, you
said, and laughed.
Dinner was a disaster.
Everybody dead drunk by the time
food hit the table. People
were having a good time, a great
time, a hell of a time, until
somebody took somebody
else's fiancée upstairs. Then
somebody pulled a knife.

But you got in front of the guy
as he was going upstairs
and talked him down.
Disaster narrowly averted,
you said, and laughed again.
You didn't remember much else
of what happened after that.
People got into their coats
and began to leave. You
must have dropped off for a few
minutes in front of the TV
because it was screaming at you
to get it a drink when you woke up.
Anyway, you're in Pittsburgh,
and I'm in here in this
little town on the other side
of the country. Most everyone
has cleared out of our lives now.

You wanted to call me up and say hello.
To say you were thinking
about me, and of the old days.
To say you were missing me.

It was then I remembered
back to those days and how
telephones used to jump when they rang.
And the people who would come
in those early-morning hours
to pound on the door in alarm.
Never mind the alarm felt inside.
I remembered that, and gravy dinners.
Knives lying around, waiting
for trouble. Going to bed
and hoping I wouldn't wake up.

I love you, Bro, you said.
And then a sob passed
between us. I took hold
of the receiver as if
it were my buddy's arm.
And I wished for us both
I could put my arms
around you, old friend.
I love you too, Bro.
I said that, and then we hung up.

Gravy

No other word will do. For that's what it was. Gravy.
Gravy, these past ten years.
Alive, sober, working, loving and
being loved by a good woman. Eleven years
ago he was told he had six months to live
at the rate he was going. And he was going
nowhere but down. So he changed his ways
somehow. He quit drinking! And the rest?
After that it was all gravy, every minute
of it, up to and including when he was told about,
well, some things that were breaking down and
building up inside his head. "Don't weep for me,"
he said to his friends. "I'm a lucky man.
I've had ten years longer than I or anyone
expected. Pure gravy. And don't forget it."

CONTRIBUTORS' NOTES

Michael Burkard's books include *My Secret Boat* (W. W. Norton, 1990) and *The Fires They Kept* (Metro Book Co., 1986). He received two fellowships in poetry from the National Endowment for the Arts and a Whiting Writers' Award in 1988. He works as an alcoholism counselor at Amethyst CDS in Oneida, New York. He also teaches creative writing at, among other places, the University of Louisville, New York University, and Sarah Lawrence College.

Raymond Carver held an international reputation as the foremost short story writer of his generation at the time of his death in 1988. He wrote five books of stories and a miscellany: *Will You Please Be Quiet, Please?* (McGraw-Hill, 1976), nominated for the National Book Award; *Furious Seasons and Other Stories* (Capra Press, 1977); *What We Talk About When We Talk About Love* (Knopf, 1981); *Cathedral* (Knopf, 1983), nominated for the National Book Critics Circle Award and runner-up for the Pulitzer Prize; *Where I'm Calling From* (Atlantic Monthly Press, 1988); and *Fires: Essays, Poems, Stories* (Capra Press, 1983). His five books of poetry include: *Where Water Comes Together With Other Water* (Random House, 1985), *Ultramarine* (Random House, 1986), and *A New Path to the Waterfall* (published posthumously by Atlantic Monthly Press, 1989). *No Heroics, Please* (Vintage, 1992), edited by William Stull, collects his early writings and uncollected prose. His work has been translated into more than twenty languages, most prominently into a six-volume *Complete Works* in Japanese by the novelist Haruki Murakami.

Tess Gallagher is a poet, short story writer, scriptwriter, and essayist. Her most recent publications are *My Black Horse: New and Selected Poems*, released in Great Britain in 1995, and *Portable Kisses*, 1996, both from Bloodaxe Books. Her books of poetry in the U.S. include *Portable Kisses Expanded*

(Capra, 1994), *Moon Crossing Bridge* (Graywolf, 1992), *Amplitude: New and Selected Poems* (Graywolf, 1987), and *Under Stars* (Graywolf, 1978). Ms. Gallagher is currently writing short stories toward a collection forthcoming from Scribner in 1997. Her first book of stories, *The Lover of Horses,* is available from Graywolf, and her essays are collected in *A Concert of Tenses* (University of Michigan Press, 1986). Ms. Gallagher is completing the third year on a grant from the Lyndhurst Foundation and will hold a chair at Whitman College as the Edward F. Arnold Visiting Professor of English during academic year 1996–97.

Cindy Goff received a Master of Fine Arts in creative writing from George Mason University in 1993. While at George Mason University, she was a poetry editor for *Phoebe* and taught composition and literature. She was the recipient of the Mary Cotton Memorial Fellowship in 1991, and a Lannan Foundation Fellowship in 1992. She currently teaches composition and developmental writing at Northern Virginia Community College in Manassas, Virginia, and at Lord Fairfax Community College in Warrenton, Virginia. Her poems have appeared or will appear in *The Quarterly, Poetry East, Spoon River Poetry Review, Surreal, Alternative Press Magazine, Poetry Motel, Mudfish, 5th Gear, Exquisite Corpse, Phoebe, So to Speak, Hyper Age,* and *The Lullwater Review.*

Marie Howe is the author of *The Good Thief* (Persea Books, 1988), which was a National Poetry Series selection. She recently edited an anthology called *In the Company of My Solitude: American Writing from the AIDS Pandemic* with Michael Klein, also from Persea Books. Howe teaches at Sarah Lawrence College in the graduate writing program and in the Warren Wilson M.F.A. writing program. Currently, she is finishing a second collection of poems called *What the Living Do.*

Lynda Hull was born in Newark, New Jersey, in 1954, and was the author of three collections of poetry, *Ghost Money* (University of Massachusetts Press, 1986), *Star Ledger* (University of Iowa Press, 1991), and *The Only World* (HarperCollins, 1995). Her work appeared in many journals and anthologies, and she taught at a number of universities, among them Brandeis, Vermont College, De Paul, and Johns Hopkins. She died in 1994, of injuries she sustained in an auto accident. Regarding her work, the critic Robert Polito has written, "Lyrical and harrowing, Hull suggests a fantasy coupling of Elizabeth Bishop and Lou Reed.... Her poems that reach out to twentieth century catastrophe track the same implosive trajectory.... Few poets of Lynda Hull's generation possess anything like her lyric gift."

Denis Johnson is the author of three collections of poetry, *The Incognito Lounge, The Veil,* and *Throne of the Third Heaven of the Nations Millennium General Assembly: Poems Collected and New.* He has also published four novels, *Resuscitation of a Hanged Man, Fiskadoro, The Stars at Noon,* and *Angels,* as well as a collection of short stories, *Jesus' Son.* He lives in Bonner's Ferry, Idaho.

Etheridge Knight began writing poetry when he was an inmate at the Indiana State Prison. His published works include *Poems from Prison* (1968), *Belly Song and Other Poems* (1973), *Born of a Woman: New and Selected Poems* (1980), and *The Essential Etheridge Knight* (1986). *Belly Song* was nominated for both the Pulitzer Prize and the National Book Award. He died in 1991 at the age of fifty-nine from lung cancer.

Joan Larkin's published collections of poetry are *Housework* (Out & Out Books), *A Long Sound* (Granite Press), and *Cold River* (Olive's Press). She co-edited the anthologies *Amazon Poetry* and *Lesbian Poetry* with Elly Bulkin and *Gay and Lesbian Poetry in Our Time* (which received a Lambda Literary Award in 1988) with Carl Morse. Her verse play *The Living* has had staged readings in South Hadley, Boston, and Cape Cod. She has taught at Brooklyn College, Sarah Lawrence, and the Goddard College M.F.A. program in creative writing. She lives and writes in New York City.

Thomas Lux teaches at Sarah Lawrence College. His most recent book is *Split Horizon* (Houghton Mifflin) and the same publisher will be bringing out *New and Selected Poems: 1975–95* in early 1997.

Jeffrey McDaniel is one of the few acclaimed performance poets to have his work appear in major literary publications, including *Ploughshares* and *Best American Poetry 1994.* He has performed his work at the 1994 Lollapalooza Festival, the Moscow Writers Union, the Globe in Prague, the National Poetry Slam, and at venues throughout the U.S. His first collection of poetry, *Alibi School,* appeared in 1995 from Manic D Press.

Jane Mead was educated at Vassar College, Syracuse University, and the University of Iowa Writers' Workshop and has taught at several schools in the San Francisco Bay area, at Colby College, and in the Iowa Summer Writing Festival. Her first full-length collection of poems, *The Lord and the General Din of the World,* was selected by Philip Levine as the 1995 winner of the Kathryn A. Morton Prize in Poetry and was published in 1996 by Sarabande Books. Her individual poems have appeared in such places as *The New York Times, Best American Poetry of 1990, American Poetry Review, The Virginia Quarterly, Ploughshares,* and *The Antioch Review.* In 1992, she received a Whiting Writers' Award.

Nancy Mitchell is a graduate of the M.F.A. Program for Creative Writing at Warren Wilson College. She is Marketing Director for Four Way Books and lives in Washington, D.C. Her poems have appeared in *The Louisville Review* and *North Atlantic Review.*

Martha Rhodes is the author of the poetry collection *At the Gate* (Provincetown Arts Press Poets Series, 1995). Her poems have appeared in such journals as *Agni, Harvard Review, Ploughshares, The Virginia Quarterly Review,* among others. She is a founding editor of Four Way Books, an independent literary press.

Cindy Day Roberts is currently a program coordinator at the Central New York Community Arts Council where she also writes and edits two newsletters, *Arts Letter,* the monthly Arts Council newsletter, and *Catalyst,* a quarterly newsletter for the Arts in Education Institute. Her poetry has been published in *Denver Quarterly, Ironwood, West Branch, The Literary Review,* and *En Passant,* among other journals and quarterlies. In recent years, she has given poetry readings at South Shore Arts, Hamilton College, and the Oneida Community Mansion House, among other places. A native of Hartford, Connecticut, she has lived in central New York for twenty-two years.

William Loran Smith is a graduate student in the M.F.A. program at Vermont College. Most recently, his work has appeared in *Kansas Quarterly, Louisville Review,* and *Omphalus,* a spoken word CD from *White Fields Press.* His book, *Night Train,* appeared in 1996 from Plinth Press.

Jean Valentine was born in Chicago and is a graduate of Radcliffe College. She is the recipient of a Guggenheim Fellowship and awards from the National Endowment for the Arts, the New York State Council for the Arts, the Bunting Institute, and from the Rockefeller Foundation. She teaches at Sarah Lawrence College and currently resides in County Sligo, Ireland. Her most recent collection of poetry, *The River at Wolf,* appeared in 1992 from Alice James Books.

THE EDITORS

Sarah Gorham is the author of two collections of poetry, *Don't Go Back to Sleep* (Galileo Press, 1989) and *The Tension Zone* (Four Way Books, 1996). Her work has appeared widely in such places as *The Nation, Antæus, Poetry, The Kenyon Review, Grand Street, The Missouri Review, The Georgia Review, The Southern Review,* and *Poetry Northwest,* where in 1990 she won the Carolyn Kizer Award. She has received grants from the Kentucky State Arts Council, the Kentucky Foundation for Women, the Delaware State Arts Council, and the Connecticut Commission on the Arts. She is Editor-in-Chief and President of Sarabande Books, Inc.

Jeffrey Skinner has published three collections of poetry, *Late Stars* (Wesleyan University Press, 1985), *A Guide to Forgetting* (Graywolf Press, 1988) and *The Company of Heaven* (University of Pittsburgh Press, 1992). His work has appeared in numerous magazines including *The Atlantic, The New Yorker, The Nation, The Georgia Review,* and *Poetry.* He has been awarded grants from the National Endowment for the Arts, the Ingram Merrill Foundation, the Howard Foundation, and several state arts councils. He is also a playwright, and two of his plays were finalists in the Eugene O'Neill Theater Conference competition. He is currently Director of Creative Writing and Professor of English at the University of Louisville.

ACKNOWLEDGMENTS

Michael Burkard. "But Beautiful" first appeared in *The Paris Review* (Fall 1990). "Your Sister Life" first appeared in *The Plum Review* (1995). "Sober Ghost" originally appeared in *Panoply* (Volume 3 #1) under the title "Katya." "The Summer after Last" first appeared in *Shankpainter* (#27, Spring 1987). "How I Shaded the Book" first appeared in *Volt* (#1). "Woman in the Red House" is published here for the first time. All poems are reprinted by permission of the author.

Raymond Carver. "The Old Days" is reprinted from *Where Water Comes Together with Other Water,* Random House, Inc., © 1984 by Tess Gallagher. "Alcohol," "Luck," and "Drinking While Driving" are reprinted from *Fires,* Harvill Press, © 1985 by Tess Gallagher. "NyQuil" is reprinted from *Ultramarine,* Random House, Inc., © 1986 by Tess Gallagher. "Gravy" is reprinted from *A New Path to the Waterfall,* Atlantic Monthly Press, © 1989 by Tess Gallagher. All poems are used with the permission of Tess Gallagher.

Tess Gallagher. "Even Now You Are Leaving," "3 A.M. Kitchen: My Father Talking," "On Your Own," "Coming Home," and "Kidnaper" are reprinted from *Amplitude: New and Selected Poems,* © 1987 by Tess Gallagher. Reprinted with the permission of Graywolf Press, St. Paul, Minnesota.

Cindy Goff. "The First Sober Morning," "I Feel Unattractive during Mating Season," "Addiction," "Drinking Beer with Sir," and "Turning into an Oak Tree" are published here for the first time. All poems are used by permission of the author.

Marie Howe. "How Many Times" and "Recovery" are reprinted from *The Good Thief,* Persea Books, © 1988 by Marie Howe. "The Promise" first ap-

Nancy Mitchell. "Love Story in Subtitles," "Runaway," and "Incognito" are published here for the first time. "The Leaving" originally appeared in *Salt Hill Journal* #2. They are used by permission of the author.

Martha Rhodes. "For Her Children," "All the Soups," "Who Knew," "A Small Pain," "His," and "Sweeping the Floor" are reprinted from *At the Gate,* Provincetown Arts Press, © 1995 by Martha Rhodes. They are used by permission of the author.

Cindy Day Roberts. "The Leopard," "Poor Zelda," "Enough," and "Let Go of It" are published here for the first time. They are used by permission of the author.

William Loran Smith. "The Family Man," "A Good Man's Fate," "Sole of Dover," and "Butchertown" are published here for the first time. They are used by permission of the author.

Jean Valentine. "American River Sky Alcohol Father," "The River at Wolf," "The Summer Was Not Long Enough," "Everyone Was Drunk," and "Night Lake" are reprinted from *The River at Wolf,* Alice James Books, © 1992 by Jean Valentine. "The Drinker's Wife Writes Back," "Forces," and "Trust Me" are reprinted from *Home Deep Blue,* Alice James Books, © 1988 by Jean Valentine. They are used by permission of the author.